Designs of Famous Utopias

MATERIALS FOR RESEARCH PAPERS

DONALD J. GRAY
Indiana University

ALLAN H. ORRICK
Rutgers University

HOLT, RINEHART AND WINSTON
New York • Chicago • San Francisco
Toronto • London

Contents

ISBN 0-03-008545-4

67890 076 19181716151413

To the Student

CONTROLLED RESEARCH

Frequently, student research papers end about where they should begin. The specialized tools of research available in the average college or university library are bewildering to the beginning student and can be mastered only through lengthy association. Most students have to spend numberless hours locating material for a possible topic and getting a sufficient acquaintance with the general subject matter area to define a satisfactory thesis for a paper of limited length. Having devoted their energies to these tasks, they allow themselves but little time to consider and fulfill the demands of the paper itself.

Since the primary purpose of the practice paper is not to provide a knowledge of the library's facilities but rather to teach the techniques of reading, analyzing, recording, organizing, and presenting fact and opinion, the idea of *controlled research* has been developed to enable you and your instructor to isolate these matters for intensive work. In other words, it is the purpose of controlled research to eliminate the difficulties you would encounter if you tried to master simultaneously the use of the library and the techniques of writing a research paper. In this pamphlet, we have gathered for your study and analysis a series of selections concerned with a common theme and have presented them in a form which gives you all the editorial information you will need to meet the conventional requirements for a paper based on printed sources. In effect, we have gone to the library for you.

Although the primary purpose of these reading selections is to afford a restricted compass within which some of the techniques of research may be practiced, the pamphlet is not intended as a substitute for the freshman handbook or research manual, and it does not explicitly discuss the basic principles of research, the specific techniques of library research, or the special mechanics of the research paper. However, the exercises, lists of topics, selected bibliographies, and lists of subjects for library papers which follow each reading selection are designed to introduce you to every aspect of preparing a paper based on written sources.

READING SELECTIONS

In the selections which follow we present a body of material dealing with the formation and structure of an ideal society. We have picked this subject because man's continuing struggle to better the milieu in which he exists, manifested by political and moral movements as well as by a literary tradition, shows that quest to have been and to be still a subject of importance to thinking people everywhere. As you read the selections you will become aware that every writer who constructs an ideal society must consider certain specific questions common to all human societies. A particular writer's answers to these questions constitute his opinion of the best of all possible designs for what present-day social scientists call *social institutions*: economics, politics, the law, communications, the family, religion, recreation, the arts, and education. Furthermore, each of the writers represented in this pamphlet has based his conception of the ideal society on one or two key ideas. These ideas not only reflect the concerns and structure of the particular society and period in which the writer lived and worked but they also determine to a great extent the author's answers to the questions he faced.

The choice of eight works excerpted here from the hundreds written on the theme was dictated by several considerations. First, with the exception of *The New Atlantis,* the picture of society each paints is complete in its details. Second, each holds an important place in the development of Utopian literature. Third, in most cases their authors would hold important places in the development of Western civilization even if they had never written utopias. Finally, because of these three reasons, all of these books as well as books about their authors are likely to be found in every college library.

As you read the selections you should try to isolate the specific questions with which each author deals and to see how the authors' common concerns relate different selections to one another. You should, in short, begin to narrow a large subject to a workable topic and to take notes on the material relevant to that topic. In our editing we have tried to preserve the main outlines of the method by which each author develops and demonstrates his key ideas. As you analyze the selections, you should try to determine what these ideas are and to use them to evaluate the writer's opinions about specific questions. In other words, you should begin to analyze, evaluate, and record the material which you will use in your own discussion of the question you are investigating.

EXERCISES

By drilling you in the techniques of investigating, recording, and organizing material from printed sources, the exercises which appear after each reading selection will lead you step by step, exclusive of the initial discovery of your material, through the process of writing a research paper. The first exercise asks you to formulate and develop a thesis sentence for a very narrow topic based on a single source. Next you are asked to construct a thesis of broader scope based first on material from a single source and then on material from several sources. After an exercise on note taking, which properly concerns the recording of evidence, there is an exercise on outlining, which provides practice in organizing evidence. The final exercise demonstrates how, using your notes and following your outline, you can develop the thesis sentence by means of example and illustration in the research paper itself. At appropriate places in this scheme, exercises are included to introduce you to the *Oxford English Dictionary* and to footnote and bibliographical form.

TOPICS FOR SHORT PAPERS

The suggested topics for short papers which follow each reading selection are designed to drill you in defining a topic and in presenting ideas and opinions relevant to it. Since any paper based on a written source involves isolating, evaluating, and organizing another writer's ideas and opinions, developing these topics will also give you practice in the basic methods of showing relationships among ideas and to the thesis sentence of a research paper. The topics can be — and at times have been — closely related to the exercises after each selection. Moreover, some of the topics

contained in the exercises require that the larger rhetorical forms be used; for example, Exercise B on page 62 asks that a paper be written by comparison, one of the several techniques by which material can be organized and presented in a research paper.

SELECTED BIBLIOGRAPHIES AND SUBJECTS FOR LIBRARY PAPERS

Should your instructor wish to present the selections in this pamphlet as a starting place for library research papers, we have followed each reading selection with a short bibliography and two suggested subjects. The bibliographies are highly selected and the subjects are broadly defined, for both are intended merely to give you a start toward investigating the general area of your subject. After reading the items in the appropriate bibliography, you should begin to narrow the subject to a workable topic and then to complete your research through further reading in material you discover for yourself.

CONTROLLED RESEARCH TOPICS

Topics for use with all of the readings appear at the end of this pamphlet. The eight selections contain enough material on each of these topics to make a paper of approximately 1,500 words. Longer papers can be written on them if your instructor wishes to send you to additional sources; or shorter papers if he wishes to restrict the number of readings.

MARGINAL REFERENCES

The page number of each word of text has been indicated by references in the margin and, when necessary, by virgules (/) in the text. These references, along with the information contained in the headnotes to each selection, give you all the information required for the documentation of your paper. You can, therefore, practice footnote and bibliographical form by documenting your paper as if you had discovered the material in its original sources. If your instructor desires, of course, all references can be to the pagination of this pamphlet.

PLATO: The Republic

Plato. THE REPUBLIC. Vol. III of THE DIALOGUES OF PLATO, trans. B. Jowett. 3rd ed. 5 vols. London: Oxford University Press, 1892.

Since The Republic *of Plato is the earliest known account of an ideal society, the history of Utopian literature properly begins with it. Plato (427-347), the pupil of Socrates and the master of Aristotle, is said to have asked first all the important questions which man has tried to answer.*

After having discussed the meaning and nature of justice at an evening party to which he was invited, Socrates (the "I" of The Republic*) repeats the dialogue to another group. He begins the discussion by maintaining that the meaning and nature of justice will be more apparent if one first imagines a State in which justice appears. The State that Socrates imagines is a self-sufficient city-state composed of all the occupations and professions required to supply the inhabitants of the city with the necessities of life. Glaucon (the "he" who asks most of the questions) objects that Socrates has not admitted luxuries into the State. Socrates meets this objection but points out that now the State has enlarged.*

II, 373   [Socrates says:] And the country which was enough to support the original inhabitants will be too small now, and not enough?

Quite true.

Then a slice of our neighbours' land will be wanted by us for pasture and tillage, and they will want a slice of ours, if, like ourselves, they exceed the limit of necessity, and give themselves up to the unlimited accumulation of wealth?

That, Socrates, will be inevitable.

And so we shall go to war, Glaucon. Shall we not? . . . And our State must once more enlarge; and this time the enlargement will be nothing short of a II, 374 whole army, which/will have to go out and fight with the invaders for all that we have, as well as for the things and persons whom we were describing above.

Why? he said; are they not capable of defending themselves?

No, I said; not if we were right in the principle

which was acknowledged by all of us when we were framing the State; the principle, as you will remember, was that one man cannot practise many arts with success. . . . And the shoemaker was not allowed by us to be a husbandman, or a weaver, or a builder — in order that we might have our shoes well made; but to him and to every other worker was assigned one work for which he was by nature fitted. . . . Then it will be our duty to select, if we can, natures which are fitted for the task of guarding the city? . . ./Then he who is to II, 376 be a really good and noble guardian of the State will require to unite in himself philosophy and spirit and swiftness and strength?

Undoubtedly.

Then we have found the desired natures; and now that we have found them, how are they to be reared and educated? . . .

[Socrates establishes that education consists of "gymnastic for the body" and "music for the soul"; the latter, which is to be taught in the formative years, includes literature.]

. . . [T]he first thing will be to establish a censorship II, 377 of the writers of fiction, and let the censors receive any tale of fiction which is good, and reject the bad; and we

---

Jowett's translation, following the conventional practice, includes references to the pages of Stephanus' 1578 edition of Plato's writings. In this selection marginal references are also to the volumes of Stephanus, as indicated in Jowett's translation.

II, 378 will desire mothers and nurses to tell their children the authorised ones only. . . ./[T]he young man should not be told that in committing the worst of crimes he is far from doing anything outrageous; and that even if he chastises his father when he does wrong, in whatever manner, he will only be following the example of the first and greatest among the gods. . . . Neither, if we mean our future guardians to regard the habit of quarrelling among themselves as of all things the basest, should any word be said to them of the wars in heaven, and of the plots and fightings of the gods against one another, for they are not true. . . .

II, 380 Let this then be one of our rules and principles concerning the gods, to which our poets and reciters will be expected to conform, — that God is not the author of all things, but of good only. . . ./[Neither are the gods] magicians who transform themselves, neither do they deceive mankind in any way. . . . These are the kind of sentiments about the gods which will arouse our anger; and he who utters them shall be refused a chorus; neither shall we allow teachers to make use of them in the instruction of the young, meaning, as we do, that our guardians, as far as men can be, should be true worshippers of the gods and like them.

. . . . .

II, 383

III, 386 Such then, I said, are our principles of theology — some tales are to be told, and others are not to be told to our disciples from their youth upwards, if we mean them to honour the gods and their parents, and to value friendship with one another. . . . But if they are to be courageous, must they not learn other lessons besides these, and lessons of such a kind as will take away the fear of death? . . . And can he be fearless of death, or will he choose death in battle rather than defeat and slavery, who believes the world below to be real and terrible?

Impossible.

Then we must assume a control over the narrators of this class of tales as well as over the others, and beg them not simply to revile, but rather to commend the world below, intimating to them that their descriptions are untrue, and will do harm to our future warriors. . . .

III, 387 And shall we proceed to get rid of the weepings and wailings of famous men? . . . Reflect: our principle is that the good man will not consider death terrible to any other good man who is his comrade. . . . And therefore he will be least likely to lament, and will bear with the greatest equanimity any misfortune of this sort which may befall him. . . .

III, 389 Again, truth should be highly valued. . . . [I]f any one at all is to have the privilege of lying, the rulers of the State should be the persons; and they, in their dealings either with enemies or with their own citizens, may be allowed to lie for the public good. But nobody else should meddle with anything of the kind. . . .

III, 392 But now that we are determining what classes of subjects are or are not to be spoken of, let us see whether any have been omitted by us. The manner in which gods and demigods and heroes and the world below should be treated has been already laid down. . . . And what shall we say about men? . . . [W]e shall have to say that about men poets and story-tellers are guilty of making the gravest misstatements when they tell us that wicked men are often happy, and the good miserable; and that injustice is profitable when undetected, but that justice is a man's own loss and another's gain — these things we shall forbid them to utter, and command them to sing and say the opposite. . . .

III, 395 If then we adhere to our original notion and bear in mind that our guardians, setting aside every other business, are to dedicate themselves wholly to the maintenance of freedom in the State, making this their craft, and engaging in no work which does not bear on this end, they ought not to practise or imitate anything else; if they imitate at all, they should imitate from youth upward only those characters which are suitable to their profession — the courageous, temperate, holy, free, and the like; but they should not depict or be skilful at imitating any kind of illiberality or baseness, lest from imitation they should come to be what they imitate. . . .

. . . . .

III, 403 After music comes gymnastic, in which our youth are next to be trained. . . . Gymnastic as well as music should begin in early years; the training in it should be careful and should continue through life. . . .

That they must abstain from intoxication has been already remarked by us; for of all persons a guardian should be the last to get drunk and not know where in the world he is. . . . But next, what shall we say of their food; for the men are in training for the great contest of all — are they not?

Yes, he said. . . .

III, 404 Then, I said, a finer sort of training [than that of ordinary athletes] will be required for our warrior athletes, who are to be like wakeful dogs, and to see and hear with the utmost keenness; amid the many changes of water and also of food, of summer heat and winter cold, which they will have to endure when on a campaign, they must not be liable to break down in health.

That is my view. . . .

Then you would not approve of Syracusan dinners, and the refinements of Sicilian cookery? . . . Nor, if a man is to be in condition, would you allow him to have a Corinthian girl as his fair friend? . . . Neither would you approve of the delicacies, as they are thought, of Athenian confectionery? . . .

II, 408　All that, Socrates, is excellent; but I should like to put a question to you: Ought there not to be good physicians in a State, and are not the best those who have treated the greatest number of constitutions good and bad? and are not the best judges in like manner those who are acquainted with all sorts of moral natures? . . .

II, 409　This is the sort of medicine, and this is the sort of law, which you will sanction in your state. They will minister to better natures, giving health both of soul

II, 410　and of body; but/those who are diseased in their bodies they will leave to die, and the corrupt and incurable souls they will put an end to themselves. . . .

. . . . .

III, 412　Such, then, are our principles of nurture and education. . . . [T]hen what is the next question? Must we not ask who are to be rulers and who subjects?

Certainly.

There can be no doubt that the elder must rule the younger. . . . And as we are to have the best of guardians for our city, must they not be those who have most the character of guardians? . . . Then there must be a selection. Let us note among the guardians those who in their whole life show the greatest eagerness to do what is for the good of their country, and the greatest repugnance to do what is against her interests. . . . And they will have to be watched at every age, in order that we may see whether they preserve their resolution, and never, under the influence either of force or enchantment, forget or cast off their sense of duty to the State. . . .

III, 413　And there should also be toils and pains and conflicts prescribed for them, in which they will be made to give further proof of the same qualities. . . . And he who at every age, as boy and youth and in mature life, has come out of the trial victorious and pure, shall

III, 414　be appointed/a ruler and guardian of the State; he shall be honoured in life and death, and shall receive sepulture and other memorials of honour, the greatest that we have to give. But him who fails, we must reject. . . .

And perhaps the word 'guardian' in the fullest sense ought to be applied to this higher class only who preserve us against foreign enemies and maintain peace among our citizens at home, that the one may not have the will, or the others the power, to harm us. The young men whom we before called guardians may be more properly designated auxiliaries and supporters of the principles of the rulers. . . .

How then may we devise one of those needful falsehoods of which we lately spoke — just one royal lie which may deceive the rulers, if that be possible, and at any rate the rest of the city?

What sort of lie? he said. . . .

. . . They are to be told that their youth was a dream, and the education and training which they received from us, an appearance only; in reality during all that time they were being formed and fed in the womb of the earth, where they themselves and their arms and appurtenances were manufactured; when they were completed, the earth, their mother, sent them up; and so, their country being their mother and also their nurse, they are bound to advise for her good, and to defend her against attacks, and her citizens they are to regard as children of the earth and their own brothers. . . .

. . . Citizens, we shall say to them in our tale, you III, 415 are brothers, yet God has framed you differently. Some of you have the power of command, and in the composition of these he has mingled gold, wherefore also they have the greatest honour; others he has made of silver, to be auxiliaries; others again who are to be husbandmen and craftsmen he has composed of brass and iron; and the species will generally be preserved in the children. But as all are of the same original stock, a golden parent will sometimes have a silver son, or a silver parent a golden son. And God proclaims as a first principle to the rulers, and above all else, that there is nothing which they should so anxiously guard, or of which they are to be such good guardians, as of the purity of the race. They should observe what elements mingle in their offspring; for if the son of a golden or silver parent has an admixture of brass and iron, then nature orders a transposition of ranks, and the eye of the ruler must not be pitiful towards the child because he has to descend in the scale and become a husbandman or artisan, just as there may be sons of artisans who having an admixture of gold or silver in them are raised to honour, and become guardians or auxiliaries. For an oracle says that when a man of brass or iron guards the State, it will be destroyed. . . .

[Socrates continues:] . . . [E]very care must be III, 416 taken that our auxiliaries, being stronger than our citizens, may not grow to be too much for them and become savage tyrants instead of friends and allies? . . . [N]ot only their education, but their habitations, and all that belongs to them, should be such as will neither impair their virtue as guardians, nor tempt them to prey upon the other citizens. . . .

Then now let us consider what will be their way of life, if they are to realize our idea of them. In the first place, none of them should have any property of his own beyond what is absolutely necessary; neither should they have a private house or store closed against any one who has a mind to enter; their provisions should be only such as are required by trained warriors, who are men of temperance and courage; they should agree to receive from the citizens a fixed rate of pay, enough to meet the expenses of the year and no more; and they will go to mess and live together like soldiers in a camp. Gold and silver we will tell them that they have from God; the diviner metal is within them, and they have therefore no need of the III, 418 dross which is current among men. . . ./And they alone of all the citizens may not touch or handle silver or gold, or be under the same roof with them, or wear them, or drink from them. . . . But should they ever acquire homes or lands or moneys of their own, they will become housekeepers and husbandmen instead of guardians, enemies and tyrants instead of allies of the other citizens; hating and being hated, plotting and being plotted against, they will pass their whole life in much greater terror of internal than of external enemies, and the hour of ruin, both to themselves and to the rest of the State, will be at hand. For all which reasons may we not say that thus shall our State be ordered, and that these shall be the regulations appointed by us for our guardians concerning their houses and all other matters? . . .

[Socrates concludes this part of the discussion by adding one final duty to the tasks of the guardians.]

IV, 423 . . . I mean the duty of degrading the offspring of the guardians when inferior, and of elevating into the rank of guardians the offspring of the lower classes, when naturally superior. The intention was, that, in the case of the citizens generally, each individual should be put to the use for which nature intended him, one to one work, and then every man would do his own business, and be one and not many; and so the whole city would be one and not many.

. . . . .

V, 449   . . . We have been long expecting that you would tell us something about the family life of your citizens — how they will bring children into the world, and rear them when they have arrived, and, in general, what is the nature of this community of women and children — for we are of opinion that the right or wrong management of such matters will have a great and paramount influence on the State for good or for evil. . . .

V, 451   For men born and educated like our citizens, the only way, in my opinion, of arriving at a right conclusion about the possession and use of women and children is to follow the path on which we originally

started, when we said that the men were to be the guardians and watchdogs of the herd. . . . Let us further suppose the birth and education of our women to be subject to similar or nearly similar regulations. . . ./ Men and women alike possess the qualities which V, 456 make a guardian; they differ only in their comparative strength or weakness. . . . Then . . . there is nothing unnatural in assigning music and gymnastic to the wives of the guardians. . . .

The law . . . which is the sequel of this . . . is to V, 457 the following effect, — 'that the wives of our guardians are to be common, and their children are to be common, and no parent is to know his own child, nor any child his parent.'. . ./You . . . who are their legislator, V, 458 having selected the men, will now select the women and give them to them; — they must be as far as possible of like natures with them; and they must live in common houses and meet at common meals. None of them will have anything specially his or her own; they will be together, and will be brought up together, and will associate at gymnastic exercises. And so they will be drawn by a necessity of their natures to have intercourse with each other — necessity is not too strong a word, I think? . . . [A]nd this, Glaucon, like all the rest, must proceed after an orderly fashion; in a city of the blessed, licentiousness is an unholy thing which the rulers will forbid.

Yes, he said, and it ought not to be permitted.

Then clearly the next thing will be to make matrimony sacred in the highest degree. . . . [T]he best of V, 459 either sex should be united with the best as often, and the inferior with the inferior, as seldom as possible; and that they should rear the offspring of the one sort of union, but not of the other, if the flock is to be maintained in first-rate condition. Now these goings on must be a secret which the rulers only know, or there will be a further danger of our herd, as the guardians may be termed, breaking out into rebellion. . . .

Had we not [Socrates continues] better appoint certain festivals at which we will bring together the brides and bridegrooms, and sacrifices will/be offered V, 460 and suitable hymeneal songs composed by our poets: the number of weddings is a matter which must be left to the discretion of the rulers, whose aim will be to preserve the average of population? . . . We shall have to invent some ingenious kind of lots which the less worthy may draw on each occasion of our bringing them together, and then they will accuse their own ill-luck and not the rulers.

To be sure, he said.

And I think that our braver and better youth, besides their other honours and rewards, might have greater facilities of intercourse with women given them;

their bravery will be a reason, and such fathers ought to have as many sons as possible. . . .

And the proper officers, whether male or female or both, for offices are to be held by women as well as by men. . . . The proper officers will take the offspring of the good parents to the pen or fold, and there they will deposit them with certain nurses who dwell in a separate quarter; but the offspring of the inferior, or of the better when they chance to be deformed, will be put away in some mysterious, unknown place, as they should be.

Yes, he said, that must be done if the breed of the guardians is to be kept pure.

They will provide for their nurture, and will bring the mothers to the fold when they are full of milk, taking the greatest possible care that no mother recognises her own child; and other wet-nurses may be engaged if more are required. . . .

A woman, I said, at twenty years of age may begin to bear children to the State, and continue to bear them until forty; a man may begin at five-and-twenty, when he has passed the point at which the pulse of life beats quickest, and continue to beget children until V, 461 he be fifty-five. . . ./Any one above or below the prescribed ages who takes part in the public hymeneals shall be said to have done an unholy and unrighteous thing. . . . And the same law will apply to any one of those within the prescribed age who forms a connection with any woman in the prime of life without the sanction of the rulers; for we shall say that he is raising up a bastard to the State, uncertified and unconsecrated.

Very true, he replied.

This applies, however, only to those who are within the specified age: after that we allow them to range at will, except that a man may not marry his daughter or his daughter's daughter, or his mother or his mother's mother; and women, on the other hand, are prohibited from marrying their sons or fathers, or son's son or father's father, and so on in either direction. And we grant all this, accompanying the permission with strict orders to prevent any embryo which may come into being from seeing the light; and if any force a way to the birth, the parents must understand that the offspring of such an union cannot be maintained, and arrange accordingly.

That also, he said, is a reasonable proposition. But how will they know who are fathers and daughters, and so on?

They will never know. The way will be this: — dating from the day of the hymeneal, the bridegroom who was then married will call all the male children who are born in the seventh and tenth month after-

wards his sons, and the female children his daughters, and they will call him father, and he will call their children his grandchildren, and they will call the elder generation grandfathers and grandmothers. All who were begotten at the time when their fathers and mothers came together will be called their brothers and sisters, and these, as I was saying, will be forbidden to inter-marry. This, however, is not to be understood as an absolute prohibition of the marriage of brothers and sisters; if the lot favours them, and they receive the sanction of the Pythian oracle, the law will allow them. . . .

And this agrees with the other principle which we V, 464 were affirming, — that the guardians were not to have houses or lands or any other property; their pay was to be their food, which they were to receive from the other citizens, and they were to have no private expenses; for we intended them to preserve their true character of guardians. . . . Both the community of property and the community of families, as I am saying, tend to make them more truly guardians; they will not tear the city in pieces by differing about 'mine' and 'not mine;' each man dragging any acquisition which he has made into a separate house of his own, where he has a separate wife and children and private pleasures and pains; but all will be affected as far as may be by the same pleasures and pains because they are all of one opinion about what is near and dear to them, and therefore they all tend towards a common end.

. . . . .

Now then, I said, I go to meet that which I liken V, 473 to the greatest of the waves; yet shall the word be spoken. . . . *Until philosophers are kings, or the kings and princes of this world have the spirit and power of philosophy, and political greatness and wisdom meet in one, and those commoner natures who pursue either to the exclusion of the other are compelled to stand aside . . . then only will this our State have a possibility of life and behold the light of day.* . . .

He said: Who then are the true philosophers? V, 475

Those, I said, who are lovers of the vision of truth. . . .

[Socrates continues:] Let us suppose that philo- VI, 485 sophical minds always love knowledge of a sort which shows them the eternal nature not varying from generation and corruption. . . . And if they are to be what we were describing, is there not another quality which they should also possess?

What quality?

Truthfulness: they will never intentionally receive into their mind falsehood, which is their detestation, and they will love the truth. . . . And is there anything more akin to wisdom than truth?

How can there be? . . .

But then again, as we know by experience, he whose desires are strong in one direction will have them weaker in others; they will be like a stream which has been drawn off into another channel. . . . He whose desires are drawn towards knowledge in every form will be absorbed in the pleasures of the soul, and will hardly feel bodily pleasure — I mean, if he be a true philosopher and not a sham one. . . . Such an one is sure to be temperate and the reverse of covetous; for the motives which make another man desirous of having and spending, have no place in his character. . . ./

VI, 487 And to men like him, I said, when perfected by years and education, and to these only you will entrust the State.

. . . . .

[*Socrates concludes his description of the ideal State by outlining the "second education" of the leaders of this state. This education includes, in addition to the music and gymnastic studied by all the guardians, training in mathematics, astronomy, and dialectic, each of which has practical as well as moral value.*]

VII, 536 All these things, then, will have to be carefully considered by us; and if only those whom we introduce to this vast system of education and training are sound in body and mind, justice herself will have nothing to say against us, and we shall be the saviours of the constitution and of the State. . . . And now let me remind you that, although in our former selection we chose old men, we must not do so in this. . . . [Y]outh is the time for any extraordinary toil. . . .

VII, 537 At what age?

At the age when the necessary gymnastics are over: the period whether of two or three years which passes in this sort of training is useless for any other purpose; for sleep and exercise are unpropitious to learning; and the trial of who is first in gymnastic exercises is one of the most important tests to which our youth are subjected. . . . After that time those who are selected from the class of twenty years old will be promoted to higher honour, and the sciences which they learned without any order in their early education will now be brought together, and they will be able to see the natural relationship of them to one another and to true being. . . .

These . . . are the points which you must consider; and those who have most of this comprehension, and who are more steadfast in their learning, and in their military and other appointed duties, when they have arrived at the age of thirty will have to be chosen by you out of the select class, and elevated to higher honour. . . .

And so, Glaucon, we have arrived at the conclu- VIII, 54 sion that in the perfect State wives and children are to be in common; and that all education and the pursuits of war and peace are also to be common, and the best philosophers and the bravest warriors are to be their kings?

That, replied Glaucon, has been acknowledged.

Yes, I said; and we have further acknowledged that the governors, when appointed themselves, will take their soldiers and place them in houses such as we were describing, which are common to all, and contain nothing private, or individual; and about their property, you remember what we agreed?

Yes, I remember that no one was to have any of the ordinary possessions of mankind; they were to be warrior athletes and guardians, receiving from the other citizens, in lieu of annual payment, only their maintenance, and they were to take care of themselves and of the whole State.

. . . . .

TOPICS FOR SHORT PAPERS

The qualities of character and intelligence that a guardian must possess
The duties of a guardian
The difference between the education of a guardian and that of an auxiliary
The reasons for the control of literature in Plato's Republic
The practice of eugenics in Plato's Republic

EXERCISE

A. One of the most efficient ways to do research on a subject is to pose one or more questions which must be answered by reference to source material. After investigation, most questions of this sort can be answered by a single statement which is called the *thesis sentence*. The proof of the thesis is the paper itself, in which the results of the investigation are presented. For example, an investigation of the status of women in *The Republic* might begin with the question: "What is the status of women in Plato's Republic?" Because the investigation will show that women were given equality with men, the thesis sentence will become: "In *The Republic* women have a status equal to that of men."

Convert one of the above topics into a question, investigate the question, and formulate a thesis sentence. Then, drawing on the selection from *The Republic* for quotations and illustrations, write a short composition which will prove the thesis.

B. Sometimes a researcher will begin his investigation with a statement rather than a question in mind. For example, the character, education, and duties of the guardians; the distinction between the guardians and auxiliaries; the control of literature; and the practice of eugenics might suggest to a reader that: *The fundamental principle of government in Plato's Republic is aristocratic.* A statement of this kind is known as a *hypothesis,* and until it is proved through investigation, it is only tentative. If, however, the investigation reveals that the hypothesis can be proved, it can become the thesis sentence of the paper. If the hypothesis is not proved or is disproved by the evidence, it will have to be revised before it can become the thesis sentence: *The fundamental principle of government in Plato's Republic is . . .* (whatever it is found to be).

Using the excerpts from *The Republic* as illustrations, prove or disprove in a paper of 750 words the hypothesis about aristocracy in *The Republic.*

C. Using the information contained in the selected bibliography for *The Republic,* write these footnotes in the order indicated:

A reference to Dickinson, p. 101
A reference to Adam, vol. I, p. 204
A reference to Oates, p. 200
A reference to Grube, p. 97
A second reference to Oates, p. 212
A reference to Myres, p. 96
A second reference to Myres, p. 204
A second reference to Adam, vol. II, p. 8
A reference to Barker, p. 179
A reference to Taylor, p. 222

Use the *MLA Stylesheet,* Rev. ed., as a guide to footnote form unless your instructor directs otherwise.

A SELECTED BIBLIOGRAPHY

Adam, J., ed. *The Republic of Plato.* 2 vols. Cambridge, 1902.

Barker, Ernest. *Greek Political Theory: Plato and His Predecessors.* 4th ed. London, 1951.

Dickinson, G. Lowes. *Plato and His Dialogues.* London, 1932.

Grube, G. M. A. "Marriage Laws in Plato's Republic," *Classical Quarterly,* XXI (1927), 95-99.

Myres, J. L. *The Political Ideas of the Greeks.* London, 1927.

Oates, Whitney J. "The Ideal States of Plato and Aristotle," in *The Greek Political Experience: Studies in Honor of William Kelly Prentice.* Princeton, 1941, pp. 187-213.

Smith, H. B. "Plato and Modern Education," *Monist,* XXXIII (1923), 161-183.

Taylor, A. E. *Plato, the Man and His Work.* New York, 1927.

SUBJECTS FOR LIBRARY PAPERS

Plato's theory about poetry (Begin by reading Book X of *The Republic*)

The Republic and the Greek idea of the city-state

MORE: Utopia

Sir Thomas More. UTOPIA, trans. Ralph Robynson; ed. with Latin text, J. H. Lupton. Oxford: The Clarendon Press, 1895.

Sir Thomas More (1478-1535), lawyer, Lord High Chancellor of England, humanist and martyr, wrote his Utopia *in Latin and published it at Louvain in 1516. The first modern account of an ideal commonwealth, its title, which means "nowhere," has been adopted by the languages of the world as a designation for all stories on the theme.*

While on a mission to Flanders as ambassador for King Henry VII of England, the narrator of the story visits Antwerp, strikes up a warm friendship with one Peter Giles, and is introduced to Raphael Hythloday, a Portuguese adventurer and philosopher. The three discuss the evil practices of the times, all of which Raphael believes due to private property; he mentions an ideal state which he had visited where everything is owned in common, and at the insistence of Giles and the narrator he describes Utopia.

119   There are in the island fifty-four large and fair cities . . . agreeing altogether in one tongue, in like manners, institutions, and laws. . . .

    There come yearly to Amaurote out of every city three old men, wise and well experienced, there to 120 entreat and/debate of the common matters of the land. For this city . . . is taken for the chief and head city. . . . None of the cities desire to enlarge the bounds and limits of their shires. For they count themselves rather the good husbands than the owners of their lands.

    They have in the country in all parts of the shire houses or farms built, well appointed and furnished with all sorts of instruments and tools belonging to husbandry. These houses are inhabited of the citizens, which come thither to dwell by course. No household/ 121 or farm in the country has fewer than forty persons, men and women, besides two bondsmen, which are all under the rule and order of the good man and the good wife of the house. . . . And every thirty . . . families have one head ruler. . . . Out of every one of these

families or farms come every year into the city twenty persons which have continued two years before in the country. In their place so many fresh are sent thither out of the city, which, of them that have been there a year already, and are therefore expert and cunning in husbandry, shall be instructed. . . . This order is used for fear that other scarceness of victuals or some other like incommodity should chance through lack of knowledge if they should be altogether new and fresh and unexpert in husbandry. . . .

    And though they know certainly . . . how much 124 victuals the city with the whole country or shire round about it does spend, yet they sow much more corn and breed up much more cattle than serves for their own use. And the overplus they part [divide] among their boarderers [neighbors]. Whatsoever necessary things are lacking in the country . . . they fetch out of the city, where without any exchange they easily obtain it of the magistrates. . . . When their harvest day draws near . . . then the Philarches [magistrates of the country]/ . . . send word to the magistrates of the city 125 what number of harvest men is needful. . . . The which company of harvest men, being there ready at the day appointed, almost in one fair day dispatch all the harvest work. . . .

    The following extracts from Robynson's first edition have been altered to conform with current standards in spelling, punctuation, and grammar; in some cases, the vocabulary has been modernized also.

135   Every thirty families or farms choose them yearly an officer. . . . Every ten officers, with all their 300 families, are under an[other] officer. . . .

    Moreover, as concerning the election of the
136 Prince,/all the officers, which are in number 200, first are sworn to choose him whom they think most mete and expedient. Then by a secret election they name prince one of those four whom the people before named unto them. . . . The prince's office continues all his life time, unless he is deposed . . . for suspicion of tyranny. . . . And that is provided that nothing
137 touching the commonwealth shall be con/firmed and ratified unless it has been reasoned of and debated three days in the council before it is decreed. It is death to have any consultation for the commonwealth out of the council or the place of the common election. . . .

139   Besides husbandry, which . . . is common to them all, every one of them learns one or [an]other . . .
140 science as his own proper craft. . . ./For their garments, which throughout all the Island are of one fashion (saving that there is a difference between the man's garment and the woman's, between the married and the unmarried), and this one continues forever more unchanged . . . fit both for winter and summer: as for these garments . . . every family makes their own. . . . For the most part every man is brought up
141 in/his father's craft. . . . But if a man's mind stand to any other, he is by adoption put into a family of that occupation which he does most fancy. . . . Yea, and if any person, when he has learned one craft, is desirous to learn also another, he is likewise suffered and permitted. When he has learned both, he occupies whether he will, unless the city has more need of the one than of the other.

    The chief and almost the only office of the magistrates is to see . . . that no man sits idle but that everyone applies his own craft with earnest diligence; and yet for all that not to be wearied from early in the morning to late in the evening with continual work like laboring and toiling beasts. . . . For they, dividing the day and the night into twenty-four just hours, ap-
142 point . . . only/six of those hours to work: three before noon . . . and after dinner, when they have rested two hours, then they work three. . . . All the void time that is between the hours of work, sleep, and meat that
143 they are/suffered to bestow every man as he likes best himself, not to the intent they should misspend this time in riot or slothfulness, but . . . to bestow the time well and thriftily upon some other good science as
145 shall please them. . . ./[S]eeing they bestow but six hours in work, perchance you may think that the lack of some necessary things hereof may ensue. But this

is nothing so. For that small time is not only enough, but also too much for the store and abundance of all things that are requisite, either for the necessity or commodity of life. . . .

    And this in Utopia the thing itself makes . . . 147 plain. For there in all the city, with the whole country or shire adjoining to it, scarcely 500 persons of all the whole number of men and women that are neither too old nor too weak to work are licensed from labor. Among them are the officials, which (though they are by the laws exempt . . . from labor) yet they exempt not themselves, to the intent they may the/rather by 148 their example provoke other[s] to work. The same vacation from labor do they also enjoy . . . [whom] the people . . . have given a perpetual license from labor to learning. But if any one of them proves not according to the expectation and hope of him conceived, he is forthwith plucked back to the company of artificers. And, contrariwise, often it chances that a handicraftsman does so earnestly bestow his vacant and spare hours in learning and through diligence so profit therein that he is taken from his handy occupation and promoted to the company of the learned.

    Out of this order of the learned are chosen ambassadors, priests, magistrates, and finally the prince himself. . . .

    Wherefore, seeing they are all exercised in profit- 151 able occupations . . . this is the cause that, plenty of all things being among them, they do sometimes bring forth an innumerable company of people to amend the highways, if any are broken. Many times also, when they have no such work to be occupied about, an open proclamation is made that they shall bestow fewer hours in work. For the magistrates do not exercise/their citizens against their wills in unneedful la- 152 bors. . . . [W]hat time may possibly be spared from the necessary occupations and affairs of the commonwealth . . . the citizens should withdraw from the bodily service to the free liberty of the mind. . . . For herein they suppose the felicity of this life to consist.

    But now will I declare how the citizens use them- 153 selves one towards another; what familiar occupying and entertainment there is among the people; and what fashion they use in distributing everything. First, the city consists of families; the families most commonly are made of kindred. For the women, when they are married at a lawful age, they go into their husbands' houses. But the male children, with all the whole male offspring, continue still in their own family and are governed of the eldest and ancientest father, unless he dotes for age; for then the next to him in age is put in his room.

    But to the intent the prescribed number of the

citizens should neither decrease nor above measure 154 increase, it is ordained that no family . . ./shall at once have fewer children of the age of fourteen years or thereabout than ten or more than sixteen; for of children under this age no number can be appointed. This measure or number is easily observed and kept by putting them that in fuller families are above the number into families of smaller increase. . . .

156 The eldest (as I said) rules the family. The wives are ministers to their husbands, the children to their parents, and, to be short, the younger to their elders. Every city is divided into four equal parts. In the midst of every quarter there is a market place of all manner of things. Thither the works of every family are 157 brought into certain houses. And/every kind of thing is laid up several in barns or store houses. From hence the father of every family or every householder fetches whatsoever he and his have need of and carries it away with him without money, without exchange, without any . . . pledge. For why should anything be denied unto him, seeing there is abundance of all things and that it is not to be feared lest any man will ask more than he needs? For why should it be thought that man would ask more than enough, which is sure never to lack? . . .

159 Moreover, every street has certain great halls set in equal distance one from another. . . . In these halls dwell the magistrates. And to every one of the same halls is appointed thirty families. . . . The stewards of every hall at a certain hour come in to the meat markets, where they receive meat according to the number of their halls.

But first and chiefly of all, respect is had to the 160 sick that are cured in the hospitals. . . ./When the steward of the sick has received such meats as the physicians have prescribed, then the best is equally divided among the halls. . . .

161 To these halls at the set hours of dinner and supper come all the whole . . . ward. . . . Howbeit, no man is prohibited . . . to fetch home meat out of the market to his own house. . . . For though no man is prohibited to dine at home, yet no man does it willingly. . . . [I]t is a folly to take the pain to dress a bad dinner at home when they may be welcome to good and fine fare so nigh hand at the hall. In this hall all vile service, all slaughtery and drudgery, with all laborsome toil and business, is done by bondsmen. But the women of every family by course have the office and charge of cookery. . . .

162 The nurses sit several alone with their young sucklings in a certain parlor. . . . Every mother is nurse 163 to her own child. . . ./Also among the nurses sit all the children that are under the age of five years. All

the other children of both kinds . . . that are under the age of marriage do either serve at the tables or else if they are too young thereto, yet they stand by with marvelous silence. That which is given to them from the table they eat, and other several dinner time they have none. . . .

They begin every dinner and supper of reading 165 something that pertains to good manners and virtue. But it is short because no man shall be grieved therewith. . . ./No supper is passed without music. . . . For 166 they are much inclined to this opinion: to think no kind of pleasure forbidden whereof comes no harm. . . .

But if any are desirous to visit either their friends 167 that dwell in another city or to see the place itself, they easily obtain license of their magistrates unless there is some profitable let. . . ./And though they carry 168 nothing forth with them, yet in all their journey they lack nothing. For wheresoever they come they are at home. If they tarry in a place longer than one day, then there every one of them falls to his own occupation. . . . If any man of his own head and without leave walks out of his precinct and bounds . . . he is brought again for a fugitive or a runaway with great shame and rebuke, and is sharply punished. If he is taken in that fault again, he is punished with bondage. . . .

Now you see how little liberty they have to loiter, 169 how they can have no cloak or pretence to idleness . . . nor [is there] any occasion of vice or wickedness, no lurking corners, no places of wicked councils or unlawful assemblies . . . so that of necessity they must either apply their accustomed labors or else recreate themselves with honest and laudable pastimes. . . .

In the council . . ./as soon as it is perfectly known 170 of what things there is in every place plenty and again what things are scant in any place, incontinent [immediately] the lack of the one is performed [completed] and filled up with the abundance of the other. And this they do freely without any benefit. . . .

. . . . .

They reason of virtue and pleasure. But the chief 187 and principal question is in what thing, be it one or more, the felicity of man consists. But in this point they seem almost too/much given and inclined to the 188 opinion of them which defend pleasure, wherein they determine either all or the chiefest part of man's felicity to rest. . . ./[T]hey pronounce no man to be so 189 foolish which would not do all his diligence and endeavor to obtain pleasure by right or wrong only avoiding this inconvenience that the less pleasure should not be a let or hindrance to the bigger or that he labored not for that pleasure which would bring after it displeasure, grief, and sorrow. For they judge it extreme madness to follow sharp and painful virtue and not only to banish the pleasure of life but also willingly to suffer grief without any hope of profit thereof. . . ./But now, sir, they think not felicity to rest in all pleasure but only in that pleasure that is good and honest. . . .

190

And they define virtue to be life ordered according to the prescript of nature. But in that that nature doth allure and provoke men one to help another to live merrily . . . verily she commands you to use diligent circumspection that you do not so seek for your own commodities that you procure others incommodities. . . .

192

[I]t is wisdom that you look to your own wealth. And to do the same for the commonwealth is no less than your duty. . . . But to go about to let another man of his pleasure while you procure your own, that is open wrong. . . .

193

Or what greater pleasure is there to be felt when a dog follows a hare than when a dog follows a dog? . . . Therefore all this exercise of hunting, as a thing unworthy to be used of free men, the Utopians have rejected to their butchers, to the which craft . . . they appoint their bondsmen. . . .

200

They neither make bondsmen of prisoners taken in battle unless it is in battle that they fought themselves nor bondsmen's children, nor, to be short, any man whom they can get out of another country, though he was there a bondsman, but either such as among themselves for heinous offenses are punished with bondage or else such as in the cities of other lands for great trespasses are condemned to death. And of this sort of bondsmen they have most store. For many of them they bring home, sometimes paying very little for them; yea, most commonly getting them for gramercy [gratuitously]. These sorts of bondsmen they keep not only in continual work/and labor but also in bands. But their own men they handle hardest. . . .

221

222

Another kind of bondsman they have when a vile drudge, being a poor laborer in another country, does choose of his own free will to be a bondsman among them. These they handle and order honestly and entertain almost as gently as their own free citizens, saving that they put them to a little more labor. . . . If any such are disposed to depart thence (which seldom is seen) they neither hold him against his will nor send him away with empty hands. . . .

The woman is not married before she is eighteen years old. The man is four years older before he marries. If either the man or the woman is proved to have bodily offended before their marriage . . . he or she/. . . is sharply punished, and both the offenders are forbidden ever after in all their lives to marry unless the fault be forgiven by the prince's pardon. . . .

224

225

Furthermore, in choosing wives and husbands they observe . . . a custom which seemed to us very fond and foolish. For a sad and an honest matron shows the woman . . . maid or widow, naked to the wooer. And likewise a sage and discreet man exhibits the wooer naked to the woman. . . ./For all men are not so wise as to have respect to the virtuous conditions of the party, and the endowments of the body cause the virtues of the mind more/to be esteemed and regarded, yea, even in the marriages of wise men. Verily so foul deformity may be hid under those coverings that it may quite alienate and take away the man's mind from his wife when it shall not be lawful for their bodies to be separate again. If such deformity happen by any chance after the marriage is consummated and finished, well, there is no remedy but patience. . . . But it was well done that a law was made . . . because they only of the nations in that part of the world are content every man with one wife apiece, and matrimony is there never broken but by death, except adultery breaks the bond, or else the intolerable wayward manners of either party. For if either of them finds himself for any such cause grieved, he may by the license of the council change and take another. But the other party lives ever after in infamy and out of wedlock. . . ./But now and then it chances where as the man and the woman cannot well agree between themselves both of them finding other with whom they hope to live more quietly and merrily that they by the full consent of them both are divorced asunder and new married to other, but that not without the authority of the council. . . .

226

227

228

Breakers of wedlock are punished with most grievous bondage. And if both the offenders were married, then the parties which in that behalf have suffered wrong are divorced from the adulterers if they will and are married together or else to whom they lust [desire]. But if either of them both do still continue in love toward so unkind a bedfellow the use of wedlock is not to them forbidden if the party is disposed to follow in toiling and drudgery the person which for that offense is condemned to bondage. . . .

229

To other trespasses there is no prescribed punishment appointed by any law. But according to the hei/nousness of the offense . . . so the punishment is moderated by the discretion of the council. . . . But most commonly the most heinous faults are punished with the incommodity of bondage. . . . For there comes more profit of their labor than of their death, and by their example they fear [frighten] others the longer from like offenses. But if they, being thus used, do rebel and kick again then forsooth they are slain as

230

desperate and wild beasts whom neither prison nor chain could restrain and keep under. . . .

233   They do not only fear their people from doing evil by punishments but also allure them to virtue with rewards of honor. Therefore they set up in the market place the images of notable men. . . .

234   They have but few laws. . . . Furthermore they utterly exclude and banish all proctors and sergeants

235 at the law. . . . For they/think it most mete that every man should plead his own matter and tell the same tale before the judge that he would tell to his man of law. . . . But in Utopia every man is a cunning lawyer. For as I said they have very few laws. . . .

238   As touching leagues . . . they never make none with any nation. . . .

243   War or battle as a thing beastly . . . they do detest and abhor. . . . And therefore, though they do daily practice and exercise themselves in the discipline of war, and that not only the men but also the women . . . [Y]et they never go to battle but in defense of their own country, or to drive out of their friends' land the enemies that are come in, or by their power to deliver

244 from the/yoke and bondage of tyranny some people that are oppressed with tyranny. . . .

248   Their chief and principal purpose in war is to obtain that thing which if they had before obtained they would not have moved battle. . . . Therefore, immediately after that war is solemnly denounced, they procure many proclamations. . . . In these proclamations they promise great rewards to him that will kill

249 their enemy's prince. . . ./[T]here is no manner of act nor deed that gifts and rewards do not enforce men unto. . . .

250   This custom of buying and selling adversaries among other people is disallowed as a cruel act of a base and cowardly mind. But they in this behalf think themselves much praiseworthy as who like wise men by this means dispatch great wars without any battle or skirmish. Yea, they count it also a deed of pity and mercy because that by the death of a few offenders the lives of a great number of innocents, as well of their own men as also of their enemies, are ransomed and saved which in fighting should have been slain. . . .

259   If they win the field, they persecute not their enemies with the violent rage of slaughter. For they had rather take them alive than kill them. . . .

266   There are diverse kinds of religion. . . . Some worship for God the sun; some the moon; some some other planet; . . . [some] a man that was once of excellent virtue or of a famous glory. . . . But the most and the wisest part . . . believe that there is a certain Godly

267 power unknown, everlasting. . . ./Him they call the father of all. . . .

270-271   [T]his is one of the/ancientest laws among them:

that no man shall be blamed for reasoning in the maintenance of his own religion. . . .

[T]hey believe that after this life vices are ex- 274 tremely punished and virtues bountifully rewarded. Him that is of a contrary opinion they count not in the number of men as one that has lowered the high nature of his soul to the vileness of brute beasts'/ bodies much less in the number of their citizens, whose 275 laws and ordinances, if it were not for fear, he would nothing at all esteem. . . . Wherefore, he that is thus minded is deprived of all honors, excluded from all offices, and rejected from all common administrations in the weal public. . . .

They have priests of exceeding holiness and, 282 therefore,/very few. . . . They are chosen of the people 283 as the other magistrates are. . . .

Both childhood and youth are instructed and 284 taught of them. Nor they are not more diligent to instruct them in learning than in virtue and good manners. For they use with very great endeavor and diligence to put into the heads of their children, while they are yet tender and pliant, good opinions and profitable for the conser/vation of their weal public. . . . 285

Now I have declared and described unto you, as 299 truly as I could, the form and order of that commonwealth, which verily in my judgment is not only the best but also that which alone of good right may claim and take upon it the name of a commonwealth or public weal. . . . Here where nothing is private the common affairs are earnestly looked upon. . . .[T]here where all things are common to every man it is not to be doubted that any man shall lack anything necessary for his private uses so that the common store houses and barns are sufficiently/stored. For there nothing is 300 distributed after a niggardly sort; neither there is any man poor or beggar. And though no man has anything, yet every man is rich. For what can be more rich than to live joyfully and merrily without all grief and pensiveness, not caring for his own living nor vexed or troubled with his wife's importunate complaints, not dreading poverty to his son nor sorrowing for his daughter's dowery? Yea, they take no care at all for the living and wealth of themselves and all theirs. . . . And yet, besides this, there is no less provision for them that were once laborers and are now weak and impotent than for them that do now labor and take pain.

TOPICS FOR SHORT PAPERS

The outstanding characteristic of the Utopians
More's debt to Plato in *Utopia*
The basis of Utopian society
Loss of personal freedom in More's planned society
Advantages of More's society to the individual

EXERCISE

After reading the three following selections, follow the instructions on page 16.

[In Voltaire's Candide, *the hero is a naïve young man who travels all over the earth and discovers its cruelty, religious bigotry, hypocrisy, and greed. At this point in the story, he and his valet Cacambo have arrived in El Dorado, Voltaire's version of Utopia, where they watch several children playing quoits.*]

126   The quoits were large, round pieces, yellow, red, and green, which cast a most glorious lustre. Our travellers picked some of them up, and they proved to be gold, emeralds, rubies, and diamonds; the least of which would have been the greatest ornament to the superb throne of the Great Mogul.

"Without doubt," said Cacambo, "those children must be the king's sons that are playing at quoits." . . .

127   The little ragamuffins immediately quitted their/diversion, leaving the quoits on the ground with all their other playthings. . . .

"Where are we?" cried Candide. "The king's children in this country must have an excellent education, since they are taught to show such a contempt for gold and precious stones."

[*Candide and Cacambo are taken to visit an old*
130 *man.*] They entered a very plain house, for the door was nothing but silver, and the ceiling was only of beaten gold, but wrought in such elegant taste as to vie with the richest. The antechamber, indeed, was only incrusted with rubies and emeralds; but the order in which everything was disposed made amends for this great simplicity.

131   [*The old man speaks to them:*] "[T]he inaccessible rocks and precipices with which our country is surrounded on all sides, has hitherto secured us from the rapacious fury of the people of Europe, who have an unaccountable fondness for the pebbles and dirt of our land, for the sake of which they would murder us all to the very last man."

[*After a stay of a month, Candide wishes to leave.*]
135 "If we remain here we shall only be as others are; whereas, if we return to our own world with only a dozen of El Dorado sheep, loaded with the pebbles of this country, we shall be richer than all the kings in Europe. . . ."

[*They ask permission to leave, and Cacambo says:*]
137 "All we shall ask of your majesty . . . is only a few sheep laden with provisions, pebbles, and the clay of your country."

The king smiled at the request, and said: "I cannot imagine what pleasure you Europeans find in our yellow clay; but take away as much of it as you will, and much good may it do you."

Francois Marie Arouet de Voltaire, *Candide*, trans. W. F. Fleming, Vol. I of *The Works of Voltaire.* 22 vols. New York: E. R. Du Mont, 1901-03.

[*More's Utopians have amassed a great store of gold and silver through exporting their surplus goods; the following excerpts deal with the use they put this treasure to.*]

For the which purpose [war] only they keep at home 172 all the treasure which they have . . . chiefly to hire therewith, and that for unreasonable great wages, strange soldiers. For they had rather put strangers in jeopardy than their own countrymen. . . ./For this cause they keep an 173 inestimable treasure, but yet not as a treasure. . . . I mean, in that they occupy [use] not money themselves. . . ./ [G]old and silver, whereof money is made, they do so use 174 as none of them does more esteem it than the very nature of the thing deserves. . . . [G]old and silver nature has given no use that we may not well lack, if that the folly of men had not set it in higher estimation for the rareness sake. . . . Therefore, if these metals among them should be fast locked up in some tower, it might be suspected that the prince and the council . . . intended . . . to take some profit of it to themselves. Furthermore,/if they should 175 make thereof plate and such other finely . . . wrought stuff, [and] if at any time they should have occasion to break it and melt it again . . . they see . . . very well that men would be loath to part from those things. . . .

To remedy all this . . . of gold and silver they make commonly chamber pots and other like vessels that serve for most vile uses, not only in their common halls, but in every man's private house. Furthermore of/the same 176 metals they make great chains with fetters and gyves, wherein they tie their bondsmen. Finally, whosoever for any offense be infamed, by their ears hang rings of gold; upon their fingers they wear rings of gold, and about their necks chains of gold; and in conclusion, their heads are tied about with gold. Thus, by all means that may be, they procure to have gold and silver among them in reproach and infamy. . . .

They gather also pearls by the sea side and diamonds and carbuncles upon certain rocks, and yet they seek not for them, but by chance finding them they cut and/polish 177 them. And therewith they deck their young infants. Which, like as in the first years of their childhood they make much and be fond and proud of such ornaments, so when they are a little more grown in years and discretion, perceiving that none but children do wear such toys and trifles, they lay them away even of their own shamefastness, without any bidding of their parents. . . .

[*H. G. Wells' traveler to an ideal commonwealth comments on gold, its uses, and its treatment in other Utopias.*]

Gold is abused and made into vessels of dishonour, 73 and abolished from the ideal society as though it were the cause instead of the instrument of human baseness; but, indeed, there is nothing bad in gold. Making gold into vessels of dishonour and banishing it from the State is

Sir Thomas More, *Utopia.* Oxford: The Clarendon Press, 1895.

H. G. Wells, *A New Utopia.* New York: Charles Scribner's Sons, 1905.

punishing the hatchet for the murderer's crime. Money, did you but use it right, is a good thing in life, a necessary thing in civilised human life . . . and I do not see how one can imagine anything at all worthy of being called a civilisation without it.

A. These three selections, together with Plato's comments on gold in *The Republic,* contain several concepts of the worth or usefulness of gold, silver, and gems. Answer each of the following questions in a single sentence which could serve as a *thesis sentence* for a short paper.

According to Voltaire, what is the natural value of gold and gems?

Why do the El Doradans use them in the way that they do?

According to More, what is the natural value of precious metals and gems?

To what does More assign man's high evaluation of them?

How do More's Utopians treat them?

What opinion about man's inherent attitude toward precious metal and gems is implied in More's discussion of them?

How does Plato treat gold in *The Republic?*

Why does he treat it the way he does?

According to Wells, why do More and Plato treat gold, silver, and gems the way they do?

According to Wells, what is the natural value of gold?

What is the reason for Wells' approval of gold?

B. Just as certain aspects of *The Republic* suggested the possibility of a broad underlying idea which could be stated as a hypothesis to be proved or disproved, the answers to the questions above suggest several possible generalizations which can be investigated by reference to two or more of the four works quoted. But since the answers are theses themselves, the broadened statement should be a thesis which can be proved without further investigation. Formulate a thesis sentence which will require evidence from two or more texts for proof, and then develop the thesis into a paper of about 500 words. Indicate by means of footnotes the exact places in these texts from which you draw your ideas and illustrations.

A SELECTED BIBLIOGRAPHY

Adams, R. P. "Designs by More and Erasmus for a New Social Order," *Studies in Philology,* XLII (1945), 131-145.

Ames, R. *Citizen Thomas More and His Utopia.* Princeton, 1949.

Campbell, W. E. *More's Utopia and His Social Teaching.* London, 1930.

Chambers, R. W. *Thomas More.* London, 1935.

Grace, W. J. "The Conception of Society in More's 'Utopia'," *Thought,* XXII (1947), 283-296.

Hexter, J. H. *More's Utopia: The Biography of an Idea.* Princeton, 1952.

Morgan, A. E. *Nowhere Was Somewhere.* Chapel Hill, 1946.

Smelser, M. "Political Philosophy of Sir Thomas More," in *Studies in Honor of St. Thomas Aquinas* (St. Louis, 1943), pp. 12-32.

Surtz, E. L. "Thomas More and Communism," *Publications of the Modern Language Association of America,* LXIV (1949), 549-564.

SUBJECTS FOR LIBRARY PAPERS

Autobiographical aspects of More's *Utopia*

Utopian social institutions and those of sixteenth-century England

BACON: The New Atlantis

Francis Bacon. THE NEW ATLANTIS, in Vol. III of THE WORKS OF FRANCIS BACON, BARON OF VERULAM, VISCOUNT ST ALBAN, AND LORD HIGH CHANCELLOR OF ENGLAND, ed. W. Rawley. 4 vols. London: R. Gosling, 1730.

Sir Francis Bacon (1561-1626), Lord High Chancellor of England, member of the English peerage, and author, is considered the founder of modern interest in inductive logic. The New Atlantis, *which Bacon began about 1624 but never finished, was published in 1627; it provided much of the inspiration for the founding of the Royal Society some thirty-three years later.*

The book opens with an account of an intended voyage from Peru to China and Japan. However, a storm drives the ship off its course into uncharted seas; finally, out of food and with much sickness aboard, the vessel arrives at the island of Bensalem. After some delay and the swearing of an oath that the members are law-abiding, the ship's company is received and quarantined in a house of strangers. The following excerpts take up the story at this point.

239-240   . . . He said; I am by office governour/of this house of strangers, and by vocation I am a Christian priest; and therefore am come to you, to offer you my service, both as strangers, and chiefly as Christians. . . . The state hath given you licence to stay on land for the space of six weeks: and let it not trouble you, if your occasions ask farther time. . . . Ye shall also understand, that the strangers house is at this time rich, and much beforehand; for it hath laid up revenue these thirty seven years: for so long it is since any stranger arrived in this part: and therefore take ye no care; the state will defray you all the time you stay: neither shall you stay one day the less for that. . . .

The next day . . . the governour came to us again . . . and when we were set, he began thus: We of this island of *Bensalem* (for so they call it in their language) have this; that by means of our solitary situation, and of the laws of secrecy, which we have for our travellers, and our rare admission of strangers; we know well most part of the habitable world, and are ourselves unknown. . . .

242   . . . We said; we well observed those his words, which he formerly spake, that this happy island, where we now stood, was known to few, and yet knew most of the nations of the world, which we found to be true,

considering they had the languages of *Europe*, and knew much of our state and business; and yet we in *Europe* (notwithstanding all the remote discoveries and navigations of this last age) never heard any of the least inkling or glimpse of this island. This we found wonderful strange. . . .

[The governor explains that long ago his nation and the other nations of the world were involved in mutual intercourse but that navigation in other countries has decayed to the point that Bensalem is visited only by accident. He begins his explanation of why his countrymen stay at home:]

There reigned in this island, about nineteen hun- 245 dred years ago, a king, whose memory of all others we most adore; not superstitiously, but as a divine instrument, though a mortal man; his name was *Solomona*: and we esteem him as the law-giver of our nation. . . . [A]mongst his other fundamental laws of this kingdom, he did ordain the interdicts and prohibitions, which we have touching entrance of strangers; which at that time . . . was frequent. . . . [F]irst, he hath preserved all points of humanity, in taking order, and making provision for the relief of strangers distressed. . . . That king also still desiring to join humanity and policy together; and thinking it against humanity, to detain strangers here against their wills; and against policy, that they should return, and discover their knowledge of this estate, he took this course: he did ordain, that of the strangers that should be permitted to land, as many (at all times) might depart as would; but as many as would stay, should have very good conditions, and means to live, from the state. Wherein he saw so far, that now in so many ages since the prohibition, we have memory, not of one ship that ever 246 returned, and but/of thirteen persons only, at several times, that chose to return in our bottoms. What those few that returned may have reported abroad, I know not: But you must think, whatsoever they have said, could be taken where they came but for a dream. Now for our travelling from hence into parts abroad, our law-giver thought fit altogether to restrain it. . . . But this restraint of ours hath one only exception, which is admirable; preserving the good which cometh by communicating with strangers, and avoiding the hurt; and I will now open it to you. And here I shall seem a little to digress, but you will by and by find it pertinent. Ye shall understand, (my dear friends,) that amongst the excellent acts of that king, one above all hath the preheminence. It was the erection, and institution of an order, or society, which we call *Solomon's* house; the noblest foundation (as we think) that ever was upon the earth; and the lanthorn of this kingdom. It is dedicated to the study of the works and creatures of God. . . . [T]his order or society is sometimes called *Solomon's* house, and sometimes the college of the six days works; whereby I am satisfied, that our excellent king had learned from the Hebrews, that God had created the world, and all that therein is, within six days; and therefore he instituting that house for the finding out of the true nature of all things, (whereby God might have the more glory in the workmanship of them, and men the more fruit in the use of them,) did give it also that second name. But now to come to our present purpose. When the king had forbidden, to all his people, navigation into any part, that was not under his crown, he made nevertheless this ordinance; that every twelve years there should be set forth, out of this kingdom, two ships appointed to several voyages; that in either of these ships there should be a mission of three of the fellows, or brethren of *Solomon's* house; whose errand was only to give us knowledge of the affairs and state of those countries to which they were designed; and especially of the sciences, arts, manufactures, and inventions of all the world; and withal to bring unto us, books, instruments, and patterns, in every kind: that the ships, after they had landed the brethren, should return; and that the breth-

ren should stay abroad till the new mission. The ships are not otherwise fraught, than with store of victuals, and good quantity of treasure to remain with the brethren, for the buying of such things, and rewarding of such persons, as they should think fit. . . ./ But thus you see we maintain a trade, not for gold, 247 silver, or jewels; nor for silks; nor for spices; nor any other commodity of matter; but only for God's first creature, which was light: to have light (I say) of the growth of all parts of the world. . . .

. . . One day there were two of our company bidden to a feast of the family, as they call it. A most natural, pious, and reverend custom it is, shewing that nation to be compounded of all goodness. This is the manner of it. It is granted to any man, that shall live to see thirty persons descended of his body alive together, and all above three years old, to make this feast, which is done at the cost of the state. . . . On the feast-day, the father, or *Tirsan,* cometh forth after divine service into a large room where the feast is celebrated. . . ./The *Tirsan* cometh forth with all his gener- 248 ation or lineage, the males before him, and the females following him. . . . When he is set, the room being always full of company, but well kept, and without disorder; after some pause there cometh in from the lower end of the room a taratan, (which is as much as an herald) and on either side of him two young lads; whereof one carrieth a scroll. . . . This scroll is the king's charter, containing gift of revenue, and many privileges, exemptions, and points of honour, granted to the father of the family; and it is ever styled and directed; to such an one, our well-beloved friend and creditor: which is a title proper only to this case. For they say, the king is debtor to no man, but for propagation of his subjects: the seal set to the king's charter, is the king's image, imbossed or moulded in gold; and though such charters be expedited of course, and as of right, yet they are varied by discretion, according to the number and dignity of the family. . . .

By that time six or seven days were spent, I was 249 fallen into straight acquaintance with a merchant of that city, whose name was *Joabin.* He was a Jew, and circumcised: for they have some few stirps of Jews yet remaining among them, whom they leave to their own religion. . . ./Amongst other discourses, one day I 250 told him, I was much affected with the relation I had from some of the company, of their custom, in holding the feast of the family; for that (methought) I had never heard of a solemnity, wherein nature did so much preside. And because propagation of families proceedeth from the nuptial copulation, I desired to know of him, what laws and customs they had concerning marriage; and whether they kept marriage well; and whether they were tied to one wife? For that where population is so much affected, and such as with them it seemed to be, there is commonly permission of plurality of wives. To this he said. . . . You shall understand, that there is not under the heavens so chaste a nation as this of *Bensalem*; nor so free from all pollution or foulness. . . . Know therefore that with them there are no stews, no dissolute houses, no curtesans, nor anything of that kind. Nay, they wonder (with detestation) at you in *Europe,* which permit 251 such things. . . ./[T]hey have also many wise and excellent laws touching marriage. They allow no polygamy. They have ordained, that none do inter-marry, or contract, until a month be past from their first interview. Marriage without consent of parents they do not make void, but they mulct it in the inheritors: for the children of such marriages are not admitted to inherit above a third part of their parents inheritance. I have read in a book of one of your men, of a feigned commonwealth, where the married couple are permitted, before they contract, to see one another naked. This they dislike; for they think it a scorn to give a refusal after so familiar knowledge: but because of many hidden defects in men and womens bodies, they have a more civil way: for they have near every town a couple of pools, (which they call *Adam* and *Eve's* pools) where it is permitted to one of the friends of the man, and another of the friends of the woman, to see them severally bath naked.

And as we were thus in conference, there came one that seemed to be a messenger, in a rich huke, that spake with the Jew: whereupon he turned to me and said; you will pardon me, for I am commanded away in haste. The next morning he came to me again joyful, as it seemed, and said; there is word come to the governour of the city, that one of the fathers of *Solomon's* house will be here this day seven-night: we have seen none of them this dozen years. His coming is in state; but the cause of his coming is secret. . . ./ 252 Three days after the Jew came to me again, and said: Ye are happy men; for the father of *Solomon's* house taketh knowledge of your being here, and commanded me to tell you, that he will admit all your company to his presence, and have private conference with one of you that ye shall chuse: and for this hath appointed the next day after to morrow. And because he meaneth to give you his blessing, he hath appointed it in the forenoon. We came at our day and hour, and I was chosen by my fellows for the private access. . . . Then he . . . spake to me thus in the *Spanish* tongue.

God bless thee, my son; I will give thee the greatest jewel I have. For I will impart unto thee . . . a relation of the true state of *Solomon's* house. . . . I will keep this order. First, I will set forth unto you the end of our foundation. Secondly, the preparations and instruments we have for our works. Thirdly, the several employments and functions whereto our fellows are assigned. And fourthly, the ordinances and rites which we observe.

The end of our foundation is the knowledge of 253 causes, and secret motions of things; and the enlarging of the bounds of humane empire, to the effecting of all things possible.

The preparations and instruments are these. We have large and deep caves of several depths. . . . [W]e use them for all coagulations, indurations, refrigerations, and conservations, of bodies . . . for the imitation of natural mines . . . the producing also of new artificial metals . . . sometimes . . . for curing of some diseases, and for prolongation of life, in some hermits that chuse to live there. . . .

We have burials in several earths, where we put divers cements. . . . We also have great variety of composts, and soils, for the making of the earth fruitful.

We have high towers; the highest about half a mile in height. . . . We use these towers . . . for insolation, refrigeration, conservation, and for the view of divers meteors; as winds, rain, snow, hail, and some of the fiery meteors also. . . .

We have great lakes both salt and fresh, whereof we have use for the fish and fowl. . . . We have also pools, of which some do strain fresh water out of salt; and others by art do turn fresh water into salt. . . . We have likewise violent streams and cataracts, which serve us for many motions: and likewise engines for multiplying and enforcing of winds, to set also on going divers motions.

We have also a number of artificial wells and fountains, made in imitation of the natural sources and baths. . . . And again, we have little wells for infusions of many things, where the waters take the virtue quicker and better, than in vessels or basins. . . .

We have also certain chambers, which we call 254 chambers of health, where we qualify the air as we think good and proper for the cure of divers diseases, and preservation of health.

We have also fair and large baths . . . for the cure of diseases, and the restoring of man's body from arefaction. . . .

We have also large and various orchards and gardens, wherein we do not so much respect beauty, as variety of ground and soil, proper for divers trees and herbs. . . . In these we practise likewise all conclusions of grafting, and inoculating, as well of wild trees as fruit trees. . . . And we make (by art) in the same orchards and gardens, trees and flowers, to come earlier or later than their seasons; and to come up and bear more speedily, than by their natural course they do. We make them also by art greater much than their nature. . . .

We have also parks and enclosures of all sorts of beasts and birds, which we use not only for view or rareness, but likewise for dissections and trials; that thereby may take light, what may be wrought upon the body of man. . . . We try also all poisons, and other medicines upon them, as well of chirurgery as physick. . . . We find means to make commixtures and copulations of divers kinds, which have produced many new kinds, and them not barren, as the general opinion is. . . .

255   We have also perspective houses, where we make demonstrations of all lights and radiations; and of all colours. . . . We represent also all multiplications of light, which we carry to great distance; and make so/

256 sharp, as to discern small points and lines. . . . We have also helps for the sight, far above spectacles and glasses in use. We have also glasses and means, to see small and minute bodies, perfectly and distinctly; as the shapes and colours of small flies and worms, grains, and flaws in gems, which cannot otherwise be seen; observations in urine and blood, not otherwise to be seen. . . .

We have also sound-houses, where we practise and demonstrate all sounds, and their generation. . . . We represent and imitate all articulate sounds and letters, and the voices and notes of beasts and birds. We have certain helps, which set to the ear do further the hearing greatly. . . . We have also means to convey sounds in trunks and pipes, in strange lines and distances. . . .

We have also engine-houses, where are prepared engines and instruments for all sorts of motions. . . . We imitate also flights of birds; we have some degrees of flying in the air; we have ships and boats for go-/

257 ing under water, and brooking of seas; also swimming-girdles and supporters. We have divers curious clocks, and other motions of return, and some perpetual motions. . . .

We have also a mathematical house, where are represented all instruments, as well of geometry as astronomy, exquisitely made.

We have also houses of deceits of the senses; where we represent all manner of feats of jugling, false apparitions, impostures, and illusions; and their fallacies. . . . But we do hate all impostures and lies: insomuch as we have severely forbidden it to all our fellows, under pain of ignominy and fines. . . .

These are (my son) the riches of *Solomon's* house.

For the several employments and offices of our fellows; we have twelve that sail into foreign countries . . . who bring us the books, and abstracts, and patterns of experiments of all other parts. . . .

We have three that collect the experiments which are in all books. . . .

We have three that collect the experiments of all mechanical arts; and also of liberal sciences. . . .

We have three that try new experiments. . . .

We have three that draw the experiments of the former four into titles, and tables. . . .

Then after divers meetings and consults of our whole number, to consider of the former labours and collections, we have three that take care, out of them, to direct new experiments. . . .

We have three others that do execute the experiments so directed, and report them. . . .

Lastly, we have three that raise the former discoveries by experiments, into greater observations, axioms, and aphorisms. . . .

We have also, as you must think, novices and apprentices, that the succession of the former employed men do not fail. . . .

. . . [W]e have two very long and fair galleries: in 258 one of these we place patterns and samples of all manner of the more rare and excellent inventions: in the other we place the statues of all principal inventors. . . . For upon every invention of value, we erect a statue to the inventor, and give him a liberal and honourable reward. . . .

TOPICS FOR SHORT PAPERS

The economy of Bensalem

The Bensalemite's view of humanity and tolerance

The material versus the mental as a rationale for Bacon's ideal society

The underlying principles of society which Bacon stresses most heavily

Some implications of these unanswered questions: How were the scientists' discoveries to be employed? How would their employment result in the ideal society?

EXERCISE

Look up the following words from Bacon's *New Atlantis* in the *Oxford English Dictionary*. Determine from their context what they meant to Bacon and write this meaning alongside the word. Are any of these meanings current today? If you know the words at all, what is the most common meaning of each for you? The page numbers refer to the original pagination of the excerpts.

     discover (p. 245)

     lanthorn (p. 246)

     stirps (p. 249)

     mulct (p. 251)

huke (p. 251)
seven-night (p. 251)
meteors (p. 253)
virtue (p. 253)
arefaction (p. 254)
chirurgery (p. 254)

A SELECTED BIBLIOGRAPHY

Adams, R. P. "The Social Responsibilities of Science in *Utopia, New Atlantis* and After," *Journal of the History of Ideas,* X (1949), 374-398.

Allbutt, T. C. "Palissy, Bacon, and the Revival of Natural Science," *Proceedings of the British Academy,* VI (1913-14), 233-247.

Ducasse, C. J. "Francis Bacon's Philosophy of Science," in *Structure, Method and Meaning,* ed. P. Henle, *et al.* New York, 1951, pp. 115-144.

Farrington, B. *Francis Bacon, Philosopher of Industrial Science.* New York, 1949.

Gough, Alfred B., ed. *New Atlantis.* Oxford, 1915.

Prior, M. E. "Bacon's Man of Science," *Journal of the History of Ideas,* XV (1954), 348-370.

Steegmüller, Francis. *Sir Francis Bacon, The First Modern Mind.* Garden City, 1930.

Sturt, Mary. *Francis Bacon: A Biography.* London, 1932.

SUBJECTS FOR LIBRARY PAPERS

Bacon's influence on later scientific thinkers
The sources of Bacon's ideas about a scientific program

BELLAMY: Looking Backward

Edward Bellamy. LOOKING BACKWARD, 2000–1887. Boston: Ticknor and Co., 1888.

Edward Bellamy (1850-1898), journalist, author, and finally social reformer, published Looking Backward *in 1888. The timely appearance of this book resulted in its overwhelming acceptance, which in turn has caused it to be called the most influential book ever written by an American.*

In 1887, Julian West was thirty years old, a member of Boston's leisure class, and a victim of severe insomnia. On May 30, 1887, he retired to his specially constructed sleeping chamber under the foundations of his house and called in Dr. Pillsbury, Professor of Animal Magnetism, who put him into a deep sleep. During the night the house burned, and West was not discovered and awakened until September 10, 2000 — one hundred and thirteen years, three months, and eleven days later — when the present tenant of the land, Dr. Leete, came upon him accidentally. The following excerpts introduce West to Boston and America at the end of the twentieth century.

57   "In general," I said, "what impresses me most about the city is the material prosperity on the part of the people which its magnificence implies."

. . . . .

66   ". . . To make a beginning somewhere, for the subject is doubtless a large one, what solution, if any, have you found for the labor question? . . ."

"As no such thing as the labor question is known nowadays," replied Dr. Leete, "and there is no way in which it could arise, I suppose we may claim to have 67 solved it. . . ./It may be said to have solved itself. The solution came as the result of a process of industrial evolution which could not have terminated otherwise. All that society had to do was to recognize and cooperate with that evolution, when its tendency had become unmistakable." . . .

77   "Early in the last century the evolution was completed by the final consolidation of the entire capital of the nation. The industry and commerce of the country . . . were intrusted to a single syndicate representing the people, to be conducted in the common interest for the common profit. The nation, that is to say, organized as the one great business corporation in 78 which all other corporations were/absorbed; it became the one capitalist in the place of all other capitalists, the sole employer, the final monopoly in which all previous and lesser monopolies were swallowed up, a monopoly in the profits and economies of which all citizens shared. . . . At last, strangely late in the world's history, the obvious fact was perceived that no business is so essentially the public business as the industry and commerce on which the people's livelihood depends. . . ."

Finally I said, "The idea of such an extension of 82 the functions of government is, to say the least, rather overwhelming. . . . [I]t was considered that the proper functions of government, strictly speaking, were limited to keeping the peace and defending the people against the public enemy. . . ."

"And, in heaven's name, who are the pub/lic 83 enemies?" exclaimed Dr. Leete. . . . "We have no wars now, and our governments no war powers, but in order to protect every citizen against hunger, cold and nakedness, and provide for all his physical and mental needs, the function is assumed of directing his industry for a term of years. No, Mr. West, I am sure on reflection you will perceive that it was in your age, not in ours, that the extension of the functions of governments was extraordinary. . . ."

"Human nature itself must have changed very 84 much," I said.

"Not at all," was Dr. Leete's reply, "but the conditions of human life have changed, and with them the motives of human action. . . ."

85 "But you have not yet told me how you have settled the labor problem. . . . In assuming the responsibilities of capital the nation had assumed the difficulties of the capitalist's position."

"The moment the nation assumed the responsibilities of capital, those difficulties vanished," replied Dr. Leete. "The national organization of labor under one direction was the complete solution. . . . When the nation became the sole employer, all the citizens, by

86 virtue of their citizenship, became/employees, to be distributed according to the needs of industry." . . .

87 "Service, now, I suppose, is compulsory upon all," I suggested.

"It is rather a matter of course than of compulsion," replied Dr. Leete. "It is regarded as so absolutely natural and reasonable that the idea of its being compulsory has ceased to be thought of. . . . Our entire social order is so wholly based upon and deduced

88 from it that/if it were conceivable that a man could escape it, he would be left with no possible way to provide for his existence. He would have excluded himself from the world, cut himself off from his kind, in a word, committed suicide."

"Is the term of service in this industrial army for life?"

"Oh, no. . . . The period of industrial service is twenty-four years, beginning at the close of the course of education at twenty-one and terminating at forty-five. After forty-five, while discharged from labor, the citizen still remains liable to special calls, in case of emergencies causing a sudden great increase in the

89 demand/for labor, till he reaches the age of fifty-five, but such calls are rarely, in fact almost never, made. . . ."

90 ". . . What administrative talent can be equal to determining wisely what trade or business every individual in a great nation shall pursue?" . . .

91 ". . . The principle on which our industrial army is organized is that a man's natural endowments, mental and physical, determine what he can work at most profitably to the nation and most satisfactorily to him-

92 self. . . ./Usually, long before he is mustered into service, a young man, if he has a taste for any special pursuit, has found it out and probably acquired a great deal of information about it. . . . The rate of volunteer-

93 ing for each trade is closely watched. . . ./It is the business of the administration to seek constantly to equalize the attractions of the trades. . . . This is done by making the hours of labor in different trades to differ according to their arduousness. The lighter trades, prosecuted under the most agreeable circumstances, have in this way the longest hours, while an

arduous trade, such as mining, has very short hours. There is no theory, no *a priori* rule, by which the respective attractiveness of industries is determined. The administration, in taking burdens off one class of workers and adding them to other classes, simply follows the fluctuations of opinion among the workers themselves as indicated by the rate of volunteering.

94 . . ./If any particular occupation is in itself so arduous or so oppressive that, in order to induce volunteers, the day's work in it had to be reduced to ten minutes, it would be done. If, even then, no man was willing to do it, it would remain undone. . . . If, indeed, the unavoidable difficulties and dangers of such a necessary pursuit were so great that no inducement of compensating advantages would overcome men's repugnance to it, the administration would only need to take it out of the common order of occupations by declaring it 'extra hazardous,' and those who pursued it especially worthy of the national gratitude, to be overrun with volunteers. Our young men are very greedy of honor,

95 and do/not let slip such opportunities. . . ."

96 "How is this class of common laborers recruited?" I asked. "Surely nobody voluntarily enters that."

"It is the grade to which all new recruits belong for the first three years of their service. . . . These three years of stringent discipline none are exempt from." . . .

97 ". . . [W]e leave the question whether a man shall be a brain or hand worker entirely to him to settle. At the end of the term of three years as a common laborer . . . it is for him to choose . . . whether he will fit himself for an art or profession, or be a farmer or mechanic. If he feels that he can do better work with his brains than his muscles he finds every facility provided for testing the reality of his supposed bent, of cultivating it, and if fit, of pursuing it as his avocation. . . ."

98 "Are not the schools flooded with young men whose only motive is to avoid work?"

Dr. Leete smiled a little grimly.

"No one is at all likely to enter the professional schools for the purpose of avoiding work. . . . [A]ny one without it [special aptitude] would find it easier to do double hours at his trade than try to keep up with the classes. . . .

99 "This opportunity for a professional training," the doctor continued, "remains open to every man till the age of thirty-five is reached, after which students are not received, as there would remain too brief a period before the age of discharge in which to serve the nation in their professions. . . ."

. . . . .

118 "You were surprised," he said, "at my saying that

119 we got along without money or trade. . . ./A system

of direct distribution from the national storehouses took the place of trade, and for this money was unnecessary."

"How is this distribution managed?" I asked.

"On the simplest possible plan," replied Dr. Leete. "A credit corresponding to his share of the annual product of the nation is given to every citizen on the public books at the beginning of each year, and a credit card issued him with which he procures at the public storehouses, found in every community, whatever he desires whenever he desires it. . . ."

120   "If you wanted to buy something of your neighbor, could you transfer part of your credit to him as consideration?" I inquired.

"In the first place," replied Dr. Leete, "our neigh-
121 bors have nothing to sell us. . . ./People nowadays interchange gifts and favors out of friendship, but buying and selling is considered absolutely inconsistent with the mutual benevolence and disinterestedness which should prevail between citizens and the sense of community of interest which supports our social system. According to our ideas, buying and selling is essentially anti-social in all its tendencies. It is an education in self-seeking at the expense of others, and no society whose citizens are trained in such a school can possibly rise above a very low grade of civilization."

"What if you have to spend more than your card in any one year?" I asked.

122   "The provision is so ample that we are/more likely not to spend it all. . . . But if extraordinary expenses should exhaust it, we can obtain a limited advance on the next year's credit, though this practice is not encouraged, and a heavy discount is charged to check it."

"If you don't spend your allowance, I suppose it accumulates?"

"That is also permitted to a certain extent when a special outlay is anticipated. But unless notice to the contrary is given, it is presumed that the citizen who does not fully expend his credit did not have occasion to do so, and the balance is turned into the general surplus." . . .

126-127   "How, then, do you regulate wages? . . . By what title does the individual claim his particular share? What is the basis of allotment?"

"His title," replied Dr. Leete, "is his humanity. The basis of his claim is the fact that he is a man."

"The fact that he is a man!" I repeated, incredulously. "Do you possibly mean that all have the same share?"

"Most assuredly." . . .

128   . . . "Some men do twice the work of others!" I

exclaimed. "Are the clever workmen content with a plan that ranks them with the indifferent?"

"We leave no possible ground for any complaint of injustice," replied Dr. Leete. . . ./"We require of 129 each that he shall make the same effort; that is, we demand of him the best service it is in his power to give."

"And supposing all do the best they can," I answered, "the amount of the product resulting is twice greater from one man than from another."

"Very true," replied Dr. Leete; "but the amount of the resulting product has nothing whatever to do with the question, which is one of desert. Desert is a moral question, and the amount of the product a material quantity. It would be an extraordinary sort of logic which should try to determine a moral question by a material standard. The amount/of the effort alone 130 is pertinent to the question of desert. . . ."

"But what inducement," I asked, "can a man have 132 to put forth his best endeavors when, however much or little he accomplishes, his income remains the same? . . ."

"Does it then really seem to you," answered my companion, "that human nature is insensible to any motives save fear of want and love of luxury, that you should expect security and equality of livelihood to leave them without/possible incentives to effort? . . ./ 133 Based as our industrial system is on the principle of 134 requiring the same unit of effort from every man, that is, the best he can do,/you will see that the means by 135 which we spur the workers to do their best must be a very essential part of our scheme. With us, diligence in the national service is the sole and certain way to public repute, social distinction, and official power. The value of a man's services to society fixes his rank in it. . . ."

. . . . .

"Here we are at the store of our ward," said 139 Edith. . . ./As we entered, Edith said that there was 140 one of these great distributing establishments in each ward of the city, so that no residence was more than five or ten minutes' walk from one of them. . . .

". . . The goods are the nation's. They are here 142 for those who want them, and it is the business of the clerks to wait on people and take their orders; but it is not the interest of the clerk or the nation to dispose of a yard or a pound of anything to anybody who does not want it." . . .

"The clerk has, then, nothing to say about the 143 goods he sells?" I said.

"Nothing at all. It is not necessary that he should know or profess to know anything about them. Courtesy and accuracy in taking orders are all that are required of him." . . .

144 . . . With that she touched a button, and in a moment a clerk appeared. He took down her order on a tablet with a pencil which made two copies, of which he gave one to her, and enclosing the counterpart in a small receptacle, dropped it into a transmitting tube.

"The duplicate of the order," said Edith . . . "is 145 given/to the purchaser, so that any mistakes in filling it can be easily traced and rectified." . . . We buy where we please, though naturally most often near home. But I should have gained nothing by visiting other stores. The assortment in all is exactly the same, representing as it does in each case samples of all the varieties produced or imported by the United States. That is why one can decide quickly, and never need visit two 146 stores. . . ./We order from the sample and the printed statement of texture, make and qualities. The orders are sent to the warehouse, and the goods distributed from there." . . .

149-150 As we walked home I commented on/the great variety in the size and cost of the houses. "How is it," I asked, "that this difference is consistent with the fact that all citizens have the same income?"

"Because," Edith explained, "although the income is the same, personal taste determines how the individual shall spend it. Some like fine horses; others, like myself, prefer pretty clothes; and still others want an elaborate table. The rents which the nation receives for these houses vary, according to size, elegance, and location, so that everybody can find something to suit. The larger houses are usually occupied by large families, in which there are several to contribute to the rent; while small families, like ours, find smaller houses more convenient and economical. It is a matter of taste and convenience wholly. . . ."

. . . . .

160 . . . "I suppose," I said, "the inheritance of property is not now allowed."

161 "On the contrary," replied Dr. Leete, "there is no interference with it. . . . [O]ur system depends in no particular upon legislation, but is entirely voluntary, the logical outcome of the operation of human nature under rational conditions. This question of inheritance illustrates just that point. The fact that the nation is the sole capitalist and land-owner, of course restricts the individual's possessions to his annual credit, and what personal and household belongings 162 he may have/procured with it. His credit, like an annuity in your day, ceases on his death, with the allowance of a fixed sum for funeral expenses. His other possessions he leaves as he pleases."

"What is to prevent, in course of time, such accumulation of valuable goods and chattels in the hands of individuals as might seriously interfere with equality in the circumstances of citizens?" I asked.

"That matter arranges itself very simply," was the reply. "Under the present organization of society, accumulations of personal property are merely burdensome the moment they exceed what adds to the real comfort. . . . Nowadays a man whom the legacies of a hundred relatives, simultaneously dying, should place in a similar position, would be considered/very 163 unlucky. The articles, not being salable, would be of no value to him except for their actual use or the enjoyment of their beauty. On the other hand, his income remaining the same, he would have to deplete his credit to hire houses to store the goods in, and still further to pay for the service of those who took care of them. . . . [T]he relatives usually waive claim to most of the effects of deceased friends, reserving only particular objects. The nation takes/charge of the 164 resigned chattels, and turns such as are of value into the common stock once more." . . .

". . . Who are willing to be domestic servants in a community where all are social equals? Our ladies found it hard enough to find such even when there was little pretense of social equality."

"It is precisely because we are all social equals whose equality nothing can compromise, and because service is honorable, in a society whose fundamental principle is that all in turn shall serve the rest, that we could easily provide a corps of domestic servants such as you never dreamed of, if we needed them," replied Dr. Leete. "But we do not need them."

"Who does your house-work, then?" I asked.

"There is none to do," said Mrs. Leete, to/whom 165 I had addressed this question. "Our washing is all done at public laundries at excessively cheap rates, and our cooking at public kitchens. The making and repairing of all we wear are done outside in public shops. Electricity, of course, takes the place of all fires and lighting. We choose houses no larger than we need, and furnish them so as to involve the minimum of trouble to keep them in order. We have no use for domestic servants." . . .

"In case of special emergencies in the house- 166 hold," pursued Dr. Leete, "such as extensive cleaning or renovation, or sickness in the family, we can always secure assistance from the industrial force."

"But how do you recompense these assistants, since you have no money?"

"We do not pay them, of course, but the nation for them. Their services can be obtained by application at the proper bureau, and their value is pricked off the credit card of the applicant." . . .

"When you want a doctor," I asked, "do you 168

simply apply to the proper bureau and take any one that may be sent?"

"That rule would not work well in the case of physicians," replied Dr. Leete. ". . . The patient must be able . . . to call in a particular doctor . . . [but] instead of collecting his fee for himself, the doctor collects it for the nation by pricking off the amount, according to a regular scale for medical attendance, from the patient's credit card."

. . . . .

170   . . . I expressed my curiosity to learn how the organization of the industrial army was made to afford a sufficient stimulus to diligence in the lack of any anxiety on the worker's part as to his livelihood.

"You must understand in the first place," replied the doctor, "that the supply of incentives to effort is but one of the objects sought in the organization we have adopted for the army. The other, and equally important, is to secure for the file-leaders and captains

171 of the/force and the great officers of the nation, men of proven abilities, who are pledged by their own careers to hold their followers up to their highest standard of performance and permit no lagging. . . .

173   "Apart from the grand incentive to endeavor afforded by the fact that the high places in the nation are open only to the highest class men, and that rank in the army constitutes the only mode of social distinction for the vast majority who are not aspirants in art, literature, and the professions, various incitements of

174 a minor, but perhaps/equally effective, sort are provided in the form of special privileges and immunities in the way of discipline, which the superior class men enjoy. These, while intended to be as little as possible invidious to the less successful, have the effect of keeping constantly before every man's mind the great desirability of attaining the grade next above his own. . . .

175   "It is not even necessary that a worker should win promotion to a higher grade to have at least a taste of glory. While promotion requires a general excellence of record as a worker, honorable mention and various sorts of distinction are awarded for excellence less than sufficient for promotion, and also for special feats and single performances in the various industries. It is intended that no form of merit shall wholly fail of recognition.

176   "As for actual neglect of work, positively bad work, or other overt remissness on the part of men incapable of generous motives, the discipline of the industrial army is far too strict to allow much of that. A man able to do duty, and persistently refusing, is cut off from all human society." . . .

180   "I should not fail to mention. . . . that for those too deficient in mental or bodily strength to be fairly

graded with the main body of workers, we have a separate grade, unconnected with the others, — a sort of invalid corps, the members of which are provided with a light class of tasks fitted to their strength. . . ."

. . . . .

"How do you carry on commerce without money?" 193 I said. "In trading with other nations, you must use some sort of money,/although you dispense with it in 194 the internal affairs of the nation."

"Oh, no; money is as superfluous in our foreign as in our internal relations. . . . There are . . . only a dozen or so merchants in the world, and their business being supervised by the international council, a simple system of book accounts serves perfectly to regulate their dealings. . . ."

"But how are the prices of foreign goods settled, since there is no competition?"

"The price at which one nation supplies another 195 with goods," replied Dr. Leete, "must be that at which it supplies its own citizens. . . ."

". . . You must understand that we all look for- 197 ward to an eventual unification of the world as one nation. That, no doubt, will be the ultimate form of society, and will realize certain economic advantages over the present federal system of autonomous nations. Meanwhile, however, the present system works so nearly perfectly that we are quite content to leave to posterity the completion of the scheme. . . ."

"Emigration is another point I want to ask you 199 about," said I. "With every nation organized as a close industrial partnership, monopolizing all means of production in the country, the emigrant, even if he were permitted to land, would starve. I suppose there is no emigration nowadays."

"On the contrary, there is constant emigration. . . . It is arranged on a simple international arrangement of indemnities. For example, if a man at twenty-one emigrates from England to America, England loses all the expense of his maintenance and education, and America gets a workman for nothing. America accordingly makes England an allowance. The same principle, varied to suit the case, applies generally. If the man is near the term of his labor when he emigrates, the country receiving him has the allowance. . . ."

. . . . .

. . . "Not only is our cooking done at the public 201 kitchens, as I told you last night, but the service and quality of the meals are much more satisfactory if taken at the dining-house. The two minor meals of the day are usually taken at home, as not worth the trouble of going out; but it is general to go out to dine. . . ."

"You seem at home here," I said, as we seated 212

ourselves at the table, and Dr. Leete touched an annunciator.

"This is, in fact, a part of our house, slightly detached from the rest," he replied. "Every family in the ward has a room set apart in this great building for its permanent and exclusive use for a small annual rental. For transient guests and individuals there is accommodation on another floor. If we expect to dine here, we put in our orders the night before, selecting anything in market, according to the daily reports in the papers. The meal is as expensive or as simple as we 213 please, though of/course everything is vastly cheaper as well as better than it would be if prepared at home. There is actually nothing which our people take more interest in than the perfection of the catering and cooking done for them. . . ."

. . . . .

223 "By the way," said I, "talking of literature, how are books published now? Is that also done by the nation?"

"Certainly. . . . The printing department . . . is 224 bound to print/all that is offered it, but prints it only on condition that the author defray the first cost out of his credit. . . . The cost of an edition of an average book can be saved out of a year's credit by the practice of economy and some sacrifices. The book, on being published, is placed on sale by the nation. . . . The price of every book is made up of the cost of its publication with a royalty for the author. . . . The amount of this royalty is set to his credit and he is discharged 225 from other service to the/nation for so long a period as this credit at the rate of allowance for the support of citizens shall suffice to support him. . . . [I]f he in the mean time produces other successful work, the remission of service is extended so far as the sale of that may justify. An author of much acceptance succeeds in supporting himself by his pen during the entire period of service. . . ."

226 "In the recognition of merit in other fields of original genius, such as music, art, invention, design" I said, "I suppose you follow a similar principle."

"Yes," he replied, "although the details differ. In art, for example, as in literature, the people are the sole judges. They vote upon the acceptance of statues and paintings for the public buildings, and their favorable verdict carries with it the artist's remission from 227 other tasks to devote himself to his vocation. . . ./Of course there are various literary, art, and scientific institutes to which membership comes to the famous and is greatly prized. The highest of all honors in the nation, higher than the presidency, which calls merely for good sense and devotion to duty, is the red ribbon awarded by the vote of the people to the great authors,

artists, engineers, physicians, and inventors of the generation. . . ."

"How about periodicals and newspapers?" I 228 said. . . .

"The people who take the paper pay the expense 231 of its publication, choose its editor, and remove him when unsatisfactory. You will scarcely say, I think, that such a newspaper press is not a free organ of popular opinion./. . . The subscribers to the paper . . . 232 elect somebody as editor who, if he accepts the office, is discharged from other service during his incumbency. Instead of paying a salary to him, as in your day, the subscribers pay the nation an indemnity equal to the cost of his support for taking him away from the general service. . . ."

. . . . .

". . . I have a tolerably clear idea of your system 249 of distribution, and how it enables you to dispense with a circulating medium. But I should like very much to know something more about your system of production. . . . What supreme authority determines what shall be done in every department so that enough of everything is produced and yet no labor wasted? . . ."

". . . The machine . . . is indeed a vast one, but 250 so logical in its principles and direct and simple in its workings, that it all but runs itself, and nobody but a fool could derange it. . . .

"Now the entire field of productive and con-/ 251 structive industry is divided into ten great depart- 252 ments. . . . Each bureau is responsible for the task given it, and this responsibility is enforced by departmental oversight and that of the administration. . . . The production of the commodities for actual pub/lic con- 253 sumption does not, of course, require by any means all the national force of workers. After the necessary contingents have been detailed for the various industries, the amount of labor left for other employment is expended in creating fixed capital, such as buildings, machinery, engineering works, and so forth. . . ./The 254 administration has no power to stop the production of any commodity for which there continues to be a demand. . . . [A]s long as the consumer cares to pay it, the production goes on. . . . If the administration doubts the reality of the demand, a popular petition guaranteeing a certain basis of consumption compels it to produce the desired article. . . ."

. . . . .

". . . To be superannuated at that age [45] and 269 laid on the shelf must be regarded rather as a hardship than a favor by men of energetic dispositions."

"My dear Mr. West," exclaimed Dr. Leete, ". . ./ the labor we have to render as our part in securing 270 for the nation the means of a comfortable physical existence, is by no means regarded as the most important, the most interesting, or the most dignified employment of our powers. We look upon it as a necessary duty to be discharged before we can fully devote ourselves to the higher exercise of our faculties, the intellectual and spiritual enjoyments and pursuits which alone mean life. . . . [I]t is not our labor, but the higher and larger activities which the performance of our task will leave us free to enter upon, that are considered the main business of existence."

. . . . .

275 . . . "We have no jails nowadays. All cases of atavism are treated in the hospitals."

"Of atavism!" I exclaimed, staring.

"Why, yes," replied Dr. Leete. "The idea of dealing punitively with those unfortunates was given up at least fifty years ago, and I think more."

"I don't quite understand you," I said. "Atavism 276 in my day was a word applied to/the cases of persons in whom some trait of a remote ancestor recurred in a noticeable manner. Am I to understand that crime is nowadays looked upon as the recurrence of an ancestral trait?" . . .

278 "[Since] the nation [became] the sole trustee of the wealth of the people, and guaranteed to all abundant maintenance, on the one hand abolishing want, and on the other checking the accumulation of riches 279 . . . nearly all forms of crime . . ./are motiveless . . . and when they appear, can only be explained as the outcropping of ancestral traits. . . ."

"Your courts must have an easy time of it," I observed. "With no private property to speak of, no disputes between citizens over business relations, no real estate to divide or debts to collect, there must be absolutely no civil business at all for them; and with no offenses against property, and mighty few of any sort to provide criminal cases, I should think you might almost do without judges and lawyers altogether."

"We do without the lawyers, certainly," was Dr. Leete's reply. . . .

280 "But who defends the accused?"

"If he is a criminal he needs no defence, for he pleads guilty in most instances," replied Dr. Leete. . . .

"You don't mean that the man who pleads not guilty is thereupon discharged?"

"No, I do not mean that. He is not accused on light grounds, and if he denies his guilt, must still be tried. But trials are few, for in most cases the guilty man pleads guilty. When he makes a false plea and is clearly proved guilty, his penalty is doubled. Falsehood is, however, so despised among us that few offenders would lie to save themselves."

. . . . .

". . . Almost the sole function of the administra- 288 tion . . . is that of directing the industries of the country. . . . We have no army or navy, and no military organiza/tion. We have no departments of state or 289 treasury, no excise or revenue services, no taxes or tax collectors. The only function proper of government, as known to you, which still remains, is the judiciary and police system. I have already explained to you how simple is our judicial system. . . . Of course the same absence of crime and temptation to it which make the duties of judges so light, reduces the number and duties of the police to a minimum."

"But with no state legislatures, and Congress meeting only once in five years, how do you get your legislation done?"

"We have no legislation," replied Dr. Leete, "that is, next to none. . . . If you will consider a moment, Mr. West, you will/see that we have nothing to make 290 laws about. . . ."

"Every town or city is conceded the right to re- 291 tain, for its own public works, a certain proportion of the quota of labor its citizens contribute to the nation. This proportion, being assigned it as so much credit, can be applied in any way desired." . . .

It had been suggested by Dr. Leete that we should 300 devote the next morning to an inspection of the schools and colleges of the city. . . .

"You will see," said he . . . "that nowadays all persons equally have . . . opportunities of higher education. . . . We should think we had gained nothing worth speaking of, in equalizing the physical comfort of men, without this educational equality."

"The cost must be very great," I said. . . .

. . . "The greater efficiency which education gives 302 to all sorts of labor, except the rudest, makes up in a short period for the time lost in acquiring it. . . . If, 305 indeed, we could not afford to educate everybody, we should choose the coarsest and dullest by nature, rather than the brightest, to receive what education we could give. The naturally refined and intellectual can better dispense with aids to culture than those less fortunate in natural endowments. . . ./Brutishness is eliminated. 307 All have some inkling of the humanities, some appreciation of the things of the mind, and an admiration for the still higher culture they have fallen short of. They have become capable of receiving and imparting, in various/degrees, but all in some measure, the pleasures 308 and inspirations of a refined social life. . . ."

"There is still another point I should mention in stating the grounds on which nothing less than the universality of the best education could now be tolerated," continued Dr. Leete, "and that is, the interest of the coming generation in having educated parents.

To put the matter in a nutshell, there are three main grounds on which our educational system rests: first, 309 the right of every man to the/completest education the nation can give him on his own account, as necessary to his enjoyment of himself; second, the right of his fellow-citizens to have him educated, as necessary to their enjoyment of his society; third, the right of the unborn to be guaranteed an intelligent and refined parentage."

. . . . .

315 . . . "How is it that you have so much . . . [wealth]?" . . .

"Let us begin with a number of small items wherein we economize wealth. . . . We have no national, state, county or municipal debts, or payments on their account. We have no sort of military or naval 316 expenditures for men or materials, no/army, navy, or militia. We have no revenue service, no swarm of tax assessors and collectors. . . . We have no criminal class preying upon the wealth of society. . . . The number of persons, more or less absolutely lost to the working force through physical disability . . . has shrunk to scarcely perceptible proportions, and with every generation is becoming more completely eliminated.

"Another item wherein we save is the disuse of money and the thousand occupations connected with 317 financial operations of all sorts. . . ./Again, consider that there are no idlers . . . rich or poor, — no drones. . . .

"A larger economy than any of these, — yes, of all together, — is effected by the organization of our distributing system. . . ."

318 "I begin to see," I said, "where you get your greater wealth."

"I beg your pardon," replied Dr. Leete, "but you scarcely do as yet. The economies I have mentioned thus far . . . are, however, scarcely worth mentioning in comparison with other prodigious wastes, now 320 saved. . . ./[F]irst, the waste by mistaken undertakings; second, the waste from the competition and mutual hostility of those engaged in industry; third, the waste by periodical gluts and crises, with the consequent interruptions of industry; fourth, the waste from idle capital and labor, at all times. Any one of these four great leaks, were all the others stopped, would suffice to make the difference between wealth and poverty on the part of a nation." . . .

340 "After what you have told me," I said, "I do not so much wonder that the nation is richer now than then, but that you are not all Crœsuses."

"Well," replied Dr. Leete, "we are pretty well off. The rate at which we live is as luxurious as we could wish. . . . We might, indeed, have much larger incomes, individually, if we chose so to use the surplus of our product, but we prefer to expend it upon public works and pleasures in which all share, upon public/halls 341 and buildings, art galleries, bridges, statuary, means of transit, and the conveniences of our cities, great musical and theatrical exhibitions, and in providing on a vast scale for the recreations of the people. . . . Even 342 if the principle of share and share alike for all men were not the only humane and rational basis for a society, we should still enforce it as economically expedient, seeing that until the disintegrating influence of self-seeking is suppressed no true concert of industry is possible."

. . . . .

"I suppose," I said, "that women nowadays, hav- 357 ing been relieved of the burden of housework, have no employment but the cultivation of their charms and graces." . . .

". . . Our women, as well as our men, are members of the industrial army, and leave it only when maternal duties claim them./The result is that most 358 women, at one time or another of their lives, serve industrially some five or ten or fifteen years, while those who have no children fill out the full term." . . .

"I understood you," I said, "that the women- 360 workers belong to the army of industry, but how can they be under the same system of ranking and discipline with the men when the conditions of their labor are so different."

"They are under an entirely different discipline," replied Dr. Leete, "and constitute rather an allied force than an integral part of the army of the men. . . ."

"The credits of the women I suppose are for 365 smaller sums, owing to the frequent/suspension of 366 their labor on account of family responsibilities."

"Smaller!" exclaimed Dr. Leete, "Oh, no! The maintenance of all our people is the same. There are no exceptions to that rule, but if any difference were made on account of the interruptions you speak of, it would be by making the woman's credit larger, not smaller. Can you think of any service constituting a stronger claim on the nation's gratitude than bearing and nursing the nation's children? According to our view, none deserve so well of the world as good parents. . . ."

"It would seem to follow, from what you have said, that wives are in no way dependent on their husbands for maintenance."

"Of course they are not," replied Dr. Leete, "nor children on their parents either. . . ./The child's labor, 367 when he grows up, will go to increase the common stock, not his parents', who will be dead, and therefore he is properly nurtured out of the common stock. . . ."

373   "One result which must follow from the independence of women, I can see for myself," I said. "There can be no marriages now, except those of inclination."

"That is a matter of course," replied Dr. Leete.

"Think of a world in which there are nothing but matches of pure love! . . ."

. . . "But the fact you celebrate, that there are nothing but love matches, means even more, perhaps, 374 than you probably/at first realize. It means that . . . the principle of sexual selection, with its tendency to preserve and transmit the better types of the race, and let the inferior types drop out, has unhindered operation. . . . Every generation is sifted through a little finer mesh than the last. The attributes that human nature admires are preserved, those that repel it are left behind. . . .

375   "You were speaking, a day or two ago, of the physical superiority of our people. . . . Perhaps more important than any of the causes I mentioned then as tending to race purification, has been the effect of untrammeled sexual selection upon the quality of two or three successive generations. I believe that when you have made a fuller study of our people you will find in them not only a physical, but a mental and moral improvement. . . ."

. . . . . .

[The Sunday following his emergence into the new Boston, Julian West listens to a sermon comparing nineteenth-century society to that of the twentieth century and setting forth the ideals of this new society; here is the end of that sermon:]

411   "Do you ask what we look for when unnumbered generations shall have passed away? I answer, the way stretches far before us but the end is lost in light. For twofold is the return of man to God 'who is our home,' the return of the individual by the way of death, and the return of the race by the fulfillment of the evolution, when the divine secret hidden in the germ shall be perfectly unfolded. With a tear for the dark past, turn we then to the dazzling future, and, veiling our eyes, press forward. The long and weary winter of the race is ended. Its summer has begun. Humanity has burst the chrysalis. The heavens are before it."

. . . . . .

TOPICS FOR SHORT PAPERS

Theoretical advantages of Bellamy's economic system

Practical disadvantages of Bellamy's economic system

The relative importance of scientific development and invention in Bellamy and Bacon

Security versus freedom as a rationale for Bellamy's ideal society

Bureaucracy in Bellamy's ideal society

EXERCISE

Take précis notes on the passages on pages 87-89, 96-99, 164, 170-171, 176, 180, 357-358, 360. (The page numbers refer to the original pagination of the excerpts.) Use three-by-five note cards unless your instructor directs otherwise.

A SELECTED BIBLIOGRAPHY

Franklin, John H. "Edward Bellamy and the Nationalist Movement," *The New England Quarterly*, XI (1938), 739-772.

Levi, Albert W. "Edward Bellamy: Utopian," *Ethics*, LV (1945), 131-144.

Madison, Charles A. "Edward Bellamy, Social Dreamer," *New England Quarterly*, XV (1942), 444-466.

Morgan, Arthur E. *Edward Bellamy*. New York, 1944.

Sadler, Elizabeth. "One Book's Influence: Edward Bellamy's *Looking Backward*," *New England Quarterly*, XVII (1944), 530-555.

Shurter, Robert L. "The Writing of *Looking Backward*," *South Atlantic Quarterly*, XXXVIII (1939), 255-261.

SUBJECTS FOR LIBRARY PAPERS

The impact of *Looking Backward* on Bellamy's contemporaries

Some conditions in nineteenth-century America which caused Bellamy to write *Looking Backward*

HERTZKA: Freeland

Theodor Hertzka. FREELAND, A SOCIAL ANTICIPATION, trans. Arthur Ransom. New York: D. Appleton and Co., 1891.

Theodor Hertzka (1845-1924), a Hungarian-born Austrian economist and agrarian reformer, wrote Freeland *in German in 1890. The book was an immediate success, creating, perhaps, an even greater impact than* Looking Backward *had two years before. It was translated into nearly a dozen languages, and local societies were formed; these, in turn, were united into the International Freeland Society with the express purpose of bringing to reality the nation visualized in the book.*

In Freeland *the announcement with which the narrative begins causes a worldwide sensation culminating in an organizational meeting the following year at the Hague. The members of the International Free Society wish to establish their community on a large tract of fertile land in an area where they will have the greatest freedom possible. The mountain district of Kenia [Kenya] in the interior of Equatorial Africa is selected as satisfying optimally both conditions. Sufficient funds having been collected, a pioneer expedition is sent to Africa under the leadership of a young engineer, Henry Ney. The selections following the announcement detail the structure of the nation which is then founded.*

1   In July 18 . . . the following appeared in the leading journals of Europe and America:

"INTERNATIONAL FREE SOCIETY.

"A number of men from all parts of the civilised world have united for the purpose of making a practical attempt to solve the social problem.

"They seek this solution in the establishment of a community on the basis of perfect liberty and economic justice — that is, of a community which, while it preserves the unqualified right of every individual to control his own actions, secures to every worker the full and uncurtailed enjoyment of the fruits of his labour.

"For the site of such a community a large tract of land shall be procured in a territory at present unappropriated, but fertile and well adapted for colonisation.

"The Free Society shall recognise no exclusive right of property in the land occupied by them, either on the part of an individual or of the collective community.

"For the cultivation of the land, as well as for productive purposes generally, self-governing associations shall be formed, each of which shall share its profits among its members in proportion to their several contributions to the common labour of the association./ Anyone shall have the right to belong to any 2 association and to leave it when he pleases.

"The capital for production shall be furnished to the producers without interest out of the revenue of the community, but it must be re-imbursed by the producers.

"All persons who are incapable of labour, and women, shall have a right to a competent allowance for maintenance out of the revenue of the community.

"The public revenue necessary for the above purposes, as well as for other public expenses, shall be provided by a tax levied upon the net income of the total production. . . .

"For the Executive Committee of the International Free Society,

"The Hague, July 18 . . ."

"KARL STRAHL.

[The expedition under Ney's supervision was successful. A site was located and named, appropriately, "Eden Vale." The following account of the initial organization of the community is taken from Ney's own journal.]

92   The fundamental feature of the plan of organisation adopted was unlimited publicity in connection with equally unlimited freedom of movement. Everyone in Freeland must always know what products were for the time being in greater or less demand, and in what branch of production for the time being there was a greater or less profit to be made. To the same extent must everyone in Freeland always have the right and the power — so far as his capabilities and his skill permitted — to apply himself to those branches of production which for the time being yield the largest revenue, and to this end all the means of production and all the seats of production must be available to everyone. . . .

95   . . . In order that labour may be free and self-controlling, the workers must combine as such, and not as small capitalists; they must not have over them any employer of any land or any name, not even an employer consisting of an association of themselves. They must organize themselves as workers, and only as such; for only as such have they a claim to the full produce of their labour. . . .

96   The committee therefore drew up a "Model Statute" for the use of the associations. . . .

[The "Model Statute" for the organization of the associations consists of ten main points:]

1. Admission into every association is free to everyone, whether a member of any other association or not; and any member can leave any association at any time.

2. Every member has a claim upon such a share of the net profits of the association as is proportionate to the amount of work he has contributed.

3. Every member's contribution of work shall be measured by the number of hours he has worked; the older members receiving more than those who have joined the association later, in the proportion of a premium of x per cent. for every year of seniority. Also, a premium can be contracted for, in the way of free association, for skilled labour.

4. The labour contribution of superintendents or directors shall, according to a voluntary arrangement with every individual concerned, be reckoned as equal to a certain number of hours of work per day.

5. The profits of the association shall be calculated at the end of every year of business, and, after deducting the repayment of capital and the taxes paid to the Freeland commonwealth, divided. During each year the members shall receive, for every hour of work or of reckoned work, advances equal to x per cent. of the net profits of the previous year.

6. The members shall, in case of the dissolution or liquidation of/an association, be liable for the con-   97 tracted loan in equal proportions; which liability, so far as regards the still outstanding amount, attaches also to newly entering members. When a member leaves, his liability for the already contracted loan shall not cease. This liability for the debts of the association shall, in case of dissolution or liquidation, be in proportion to the claim of the liable member upon the existing property.

7. The highest authority of the association is the general meeting, in which every member possesses an equal active and passive vote. The general meeting carries its motions by a simple majority of votes; a majority of three-fourths is required for the alteration of statutes, dissolution, or liquidation.

8. The general meeting exercises its rights either directly as such, or through its elected functionaries, who are responsible to it.

9. The management of the business of the association is placed in the hands of a directorate of x members, elected for x years by the general meeting, but their appointment can be at any time rescinded. The subordinate business functionaries are nominated by the directorate; but the fixing of the salaries — measured in hours of work — of these functionaries is the business of the general assembly on the proposition of the directorate.

10. The general meeting annually elects a council of inspection consisting of x members, to inspect the books and take note of the manner in which the business is conducted, and to furnish periodical reports.

.   .   .   .   .

The buying and selling of all conceivable products   107 and articles of merchandise in Freeland was carried on in large halls and warehouses, which were under the management of the community. No one was forbidden to buy and sell where he pleased, but these public magazines offered such enormous advantages that everyone who did not wish to suffer loss made use of them. No fee was charged for storing or manipulation, as it was quite immaterial, in a country where everyone consumed in proportion to his production. . . .

The fundamental laws were thus expressed: 137

1. Every inhabitant of Freeland has an equal and inalienable claim upon the whole of the land, and upon the means of production accumulated by the community.

2. Women, children, old men, and men incapable of work, have a right to a competent maintenance, fairly proportionate to the level of the average wealth of the community.

3. No one can be hindered from the active exercise of his own free individual will, so long as he does not infringe upon the rights of others.

4. Public affairs are to be administered as shall be determined by all the adult (above twenty years of age) inhabitants of Freeland, without distinction of sex, who shall all possess an equal active and passive right of vote and of election in all matters that affect the commonwealth.

5. Both the legislative and the executive authority shall be divided into departments, and in such a manner that the whole of the electors shall choose special representatives for the principal public departments, who shall give their decisions apart and watch over the action of the administrative boards of the respective departments. . . .

138   With reference to the right of maintenance given to women, children, old men, and men incapable of working, by the second section, it may be remarked that this was regarded, in the spirit of our principles, as a corollary from the truth that the wealth of the civilised man is not the product of his own individual capabilities, but is the result of the intellectual labour of numberless previous generations, *whose bequest belongs as much to the weak and helpless as to the strong and capable.* . . . That this heritage would be unproductive without the labour of us who are strong is true, and it would be unfair — nay, foolish and impracticable — for our weaker brethren to claim an *equal* share. But they have a right to claim a fraternal participation — not merely a charitable one, but one based upon their right of inheritance — in the rich profits won from the common heritage, even though it be by *our* labour solely. . . .

139   So much as to the right of maintenance in general. As to the provision for women in particular, it was considered that woman was unfitted by her physical and psychical characteristics for an active struggle for existence; but was destined, on the one hand, to the function of propagating the human race, and, on the other hand, to that of beautifying and refining life. . . .

140   Happiness and dignity, as well as the future salvation of humanity, equally demanded that woman should be delivered from the dishonourable necessity of seeing in her husband a provider, in marriage the only refuge from material need. . . . [Her] duties do not lie in the kitchen and the wardrobe, but in the cultivation of the beautiful in the adult generation on the one hand, and of the intellectual and physical development of the young on the other. Therefore, in the interests not only of herself, but also of man, and in particular of the future race, woman must be altogether withdrawn from the struggle for the necessaries of life; she must be no wheel in the bread-earning machinery, she must be a jewel in the heart of humanity. Only one kind of "work" is appropriate to woman — that of the education of children and, at most, the care of the sick and infirm. . . .

Not only had the single woman or the widow a 141 right to a maintenance, but the married woman also had a similar right, though only to one-half the amount. This right was based upon the principle that even the wife ought not to be thrown upon the husband for maintenance and made dependent upon him. . . .

As the constituent assembly retained the twelve- 144 fold division of the governing authority, there were henceforth in Freeland . . . twelve different consultative, determining, and supervising assemblies, elected by the whole people. . . . These twelve assemblies/ were elected by the whole of the electors, each elector 145 having the right to give an equal vote in all the elections; but the distribution of the constituencies was different. . . . Some of these elections. . . . took place according to residence; the elections in other cases according to calling. For the latter purpose, the whole of the inhabitants of Freeland were divided, according to their callings, into larger or smaller constituencies, each of which elected one or more deputies in proportion to its numbers. . . .

The natural result of this organisation was that every inhabitant of Freeland confined his attention to those public affairs which he understood, or thought he understood. . . ./And this, again, had as a conse- 146 quence . . . that every branch of the public administration was in the hands of the most expert specialists, and the best qualified men in all Freeland. . . .

[Twenty-five years after the founding of Freeland, difficulties with a native king, Negus John V., caused consternation in Europe and brought diplomats from the major nations to Freeland to discuss a solution to the problem. Among these European diplomats was one Prince Falieri and his son Carlo, ambassadors from Italy. The following excerpts are from Carlo's letters to a friend in his homeland.]

". . . It seems to me that you have some ten or 193 twelve dwelling-rooms. It is true the floor is of marble, but it must be swept. Everywhere I see heavy carpets — who keeps these clean? In a word, who does/the 194 coarser work in the comfortably furnished house, which one can see at a glance is kept most carefully in order?"

". . . The household work is done on the basis of

a common tarrif without any trouble on our part. . . . The association possesses duplicates of the house-keys and room-keys of all the houses that it serves. Early in the morning, when we are most of us still asleep, its messengers come noiselessly, take the clothing that has to be cleaned — or rather that has to be exchanged — for we Freelanders never wear the same garment on two successive days . . . put the clean clothes in the proper place, get ready the baths . . . clean the outer spaces and some of the rooms, take away the carpets, and disappear before most of us have had any knowledge of their presence. . . . It is almost all done by machinery. . . .

195   "A little later the workers of the association reappear in order to clean the rest of the rooms, to lay the carpets in their places, and prepare everything in the kitchen and the breakfast-room for breakfast. And so these people come and go several times during the day, as often as is agreed upon, in order to see that all is right. . . .

197   ". . . Whilst we were at table [Mrs. Ney said] the Food Association brought in quick succession the dishes which had been ordered, in part quite ready, in part — as, e.g., the roast meat and the vegetables — prepared but not cooked. The food that was ready was placed in the respective compartments of the cupboard from the corridor; a member of the association cooked

198 the meat and/vegetables in a kitchen at the back of the house, furnished also with electrical cooking apparatus. . . . Washing the dishes, &c., is the business of the association, as is also the attendance at table if it is required." . . .

203   . . . As I was curious to see how the world-renowned Freeland benevolence . . . dealt with the sick poor in its own country, I asked David to take me to at least one hospital. "I can show you a hospital as little as I can a prison or a barracks, in Eden Vale, for the very simple reason that we do not possess one in all Freeland," was his answer.

"The absence of prisons and barracks I can understand; we knew that you Freelanders can manage without criminal laws or a military administration; but — so I thought — sickness must exist here: that has nothing to do with your social institutions!"

"Your last sentence I cannot unconditionally assent to," said Mr. Ney, joining in our conversation.
204 "Even diseases have decreased/under the influence of our social institutions. It is true they have not disappeared — we have sick in Freeland — but no poor sick, for we have no poor at all, either sick or sound. . . . We certainly have institutions in which sick persons can, at good prices, procure special and careful treatment, and they are largely patronised, particularly in

cases requiring surgical operations; but they are private institutions. . . ."

David further told me that in Freeland the physi- 205 cian is not paid by the patient, but is a public official, as is also the apothecary. The study of medicine is nevertheless as free in the universities here as any other study, and no one is prevented from practising as a physician because he may not have undergone an examination or passed through a university. . . . On the other hand, however, the commonwealth exercises the right of entrusting the care and health and sanitation to certain paid officials, as in every other kind of public service. . . . Anyone who fails to get proposed *may* practise medicine, but as the public knows that the most skillful are always chosen [as public officials] with the utmost conscientiousness conceivable, this liberty to practise is of no value. . . .

Of course I have not neglected the opportunity 216 of observing the people of Freeland at their work, both in the field and in the factory. . . . No dirty, exhausting manual toil; the most ingenious apparatus performs for the human worker everything that is really unpleasant; man has for the most part merely to superintend his never-wearing iron slaves. . . .

But all these arrangements . . . did not excite my 218 admiration and astonishment so much as the buoyant and — in the best sense of the word — childlike delight and gladness with which the Freelanders enjoyed not merely their pleasures, but their whole life. . . . "Whence do you get all this reflected splendour of 219 sunny joyousness?" I asked David.

"It is the natural result of the serene absence of care which we all enjoy," was his answer. . . . It is not because we are richer, nor even because we are all well-off, but because we — that is, every individual among us — possess the absolute certainty of continuing to be well-off. Here one *cannot* become poor, for everyone has an inalienable right to his share of the incalculable wealth of the community. . . ."

"And are you not afraid," I interposed, "that this absence of care will eventually put an end to that upon which you rely — that is, to progress? Hitherto at least want and care have been the strongest incentives to human activity. . . . Do you believe that want can completely disappear from off the face of the earth without taking progress with it?"

"We not only believe that," was his answer, "but we know it. . . . To struggle for existence is/the in- 220 exorable command, upon the observance of which nature has made progress . . . to depend. . . . Even we have to struggle for existence; for what we require does not fall into our lap without effort and labour. Yet not *opposed* but *side by side* do we stand in our struggle; and it is on this very account that the result is never doubtful to us. . . ."

221   "But," I asked, "what will prompt men to struggle in the cause of progress when want has lost its sting?"

    "Singular question! . . . As if want had ever been the sole, or even the principal, spring of human progress! . . ."

226   . . . I recalled by accident at this very moment a conversation I had had with the elder Ney about savings and insurance in Freeland. . . . I asked David, "Why do men save in a country in which everyone can reckon with certainty upon a constantly increasing return for his industry, and in which even those who are incapable of work are protected not merely against material want, but even against the lack of higher enjoyments? Does not this thrift prove that anxiety for the morrow is not after all quite unknown here?"

227   ". . . The object of this saving is to provide for the future out of the superfluity of the present; and certainly it follows from this that a certain kind of care for the morrow is very well known among us also. The distinction between our saving and the anxious thrift of other people lies merely here, that our saving is intended not to guard us against want, but simply against the danger of a future diminution of the standard of our accustomed enjoyments. . . . We know no 'care' so far as a *fear* concerning the morrow is implied by the word; but our whole public and private life is pervaded by *foresight,* in the sense of making precautionary arrangements to-day in order that the needs of to-

228 morrow may be met. . . ./An existence altogether worthy of man, participation in all that the highest culture makes *necessary* — that we guarantee to all who live in our midst, even when they have left off working. . . .

230   . . . Accompanied by David, I first visited one of the many kindergartens. . . . The children sang, danced, indulged in all sorts of fun and frolic, looked at picture-books which were explained to them, listened sometimes to fairy-tales and sometimes to instructive narratives, and played games. . . . In general the Freeland

231 mothers prefer to have their children with/them at home; only when they leave home or pay a visit, or have anything to attend to, do they take their little ones to the nearest kindergarten and fetch them away on their return. . . .

    After the kindergarten came the elementary school. . . . The teaching is entirely in the hands of women, married or unmarried; only gymnastics and swimming are taught by men to the boys. These two subjects occupy both boys and girls an hour every day. . . .

    We next went to the middle schools, in which boys and girls of from ten to sixteen years are taught apart, the former solely by men, the latter partly by women. Here still greater attention is paid to bodily exercises of all kinds. . . .

232   I learnt that, up to this age, the instruction given to all the children of Freeland is the same, except that among the girls less time is given to bodily exercises and more to musical training. At sixteen years of age begins the differentiation of the training of the sexes, and also the preparation of the boys for their several vocations. The girls either remain at home, and there complete their education in those arts and branches of knowledge, the rudimental preparation for which they have already received; or they are sent as pupil-daughters, with the same view, to the house of some highly cultured and intellectually gifted woman. Others enter the pedagogic training institutions, where they are trained as teachers, or they hear a course of lectures on nursing, or devote themselves to aesthetics, art, &c.

    The boys, on the other hand, are distributed among the various higher educational institutions. Most of them attend the industrial and commercial technical institutions, where they spend a year or two in a scientific and practical preparation for the various branches of commerce and industry. Every Freeland worker passes through one of these institutions, whether he intends to be agriculturist, spinner, metal-worker, or what not. There is a double object aimed at in this: first, to make every worker, without distinction, famil-

233 iar/with the whole circle of knowledge and practice connected with his occupation; and next to place him in the position of being able to employ himself profitably, if he chooses to do so, in several branches of production. . . .[B]y this means there can be brought about that marvellous equilibrium in the most diverse sources of income which is the foundation of the social order of the country.

    Young persons who have given evidence of possessing superior intellectual ability attend the universities, in which Freeland's professors, the high government officials, physicians, technicians, &c., are educated; or the richly endowed academies of art, which send forth the architects, sculptors, painters, and musicians of the country. Even in all these educational institutions great importance is attached to physical as well as to intellectual development. . . .

237   . . . We then discussed several other topics connected with the education of the young; and I took occasion to ask how it was that the before-mentioned voluntary insurance against old age and death in Freeland was effected on behalf of only the insurer himself and his wife, and not his children. . . .

238   "The reason," explained David, "lies here; the

children are already sufficiently provided for — as sufficiently as are those who are unable to work, and the widows. . . . What we bequeath to our children, and bequeath it in all cases, is the immense treasure of the powers and wealth of the commonwealth delivered into their care and disposition. . . ."

"But," I interposed, "suppose a child is or becomes incapable of work?"

"If he is so from childhood, then the forty per cent. of the maintenance-unit, to which in such a case he has a right, is abundantly sufficient to meet all his requirements, for he neither can nor should have an independent household. If he *becomes* incapable of work, after he has set up a household and perhaps has children of his own, it would be his own, not his parents' fault, if he had neglected to provide for this emergency — assuming, of course, that he considered it necessary to make such provision." . . .

240 . . . "May I, in this connection, ask how you deal with the right of inheritance in general, and of inheritance of real property in particular? For here, in property in houses there seems to me to be a rock upon which your general principles as to property in land might be wrecked. It is one of the fundamental principles of your organisation that no one can have a right of property in land; but houses — if I have been rightly informed — are private property. How do you reconcile these things?"

"Everyone," answered David, "can dispose freely of his own property, at death as in life. The right of bequest is free and unqualified; but it must be noted that between husband and wife there is an absolute community of goods, whence it follows that only the survivor can definitely dispose of the common property. . . .

241 "Now, in the exercise of my right of usufruct of a definite plot of ground, I have inseparably connected with this plot something over which I have not merely the right of usufruct, but also the right of property — namely, a house. Consequently my right of usufruct passes over to the person to whom — whether gratuitously or not — I transfer my right of property in the house. Therefore I can sell, or bequeath, or give away my house without being prevented from doing so by the fact that I have no right of property in the building-site.

. . . . .

255 "But undertakership is not forbidden in Freeland [said the director of the Bank]. No one would hinder you from opening a factory here and attempting to hire workers to carry it on for wages. But in the first place you would have to offer the workers at least as much as the average earnings of labour in Freeland; and in

the second place it is questionable if you would find any who would place themselves under your orders. That, as a matter of fact, no such case has occurred for the past eighteen years — that even our greatest technical reformers, in possession of the most valuable inventions, have without exception preferred to act not as undertakers, but as organisers of free associations — this is due simply to the superiority of free over servile labour. It has been found that the same inventors are able to accomplish a great deal more with free workers who are stimulated by self-interest, than with wage-earners who, in spite of constant oversight, can only be induced to give a mechanical attention to their tasks. . . .

258 "Just as little do we forbid interest. No one in Freeland will prevent you from asking as high a rate of interest as you please; only you will find no one willing to pay it you, because everyone can get as much capital as he needs without interest. . . .

259 ". . .[W]ith us, every increase in production must be equably distributed among all, the problem as to how the saver profits from the employment of his capital solves itself. . . .[T]hanks to our institutions, 260 the/increase of profit effected in any locality is immediately distributed over all localities and all kinds of production. . . .

262 "You see, it is exactly the same with interest as with the undertaker's gains and with ground-rent: the guaranteed right of association saves the worker from the necessity of handing over a part of the proceeds of his production to a third person under any plea whatever. Interest disappears of itself, just like profit and rent, for the sole but sufficient reason that the freely associated worker is his own capitalist, as well as his own undertaker and landlord. Or, if one will put it so, *interest, profit, and rent remain, but they are not separated from wages, with which they combine to form a single and indivisible return for labour.*" . . .

262 I now addressed to Mr. Clark [the director of the Bank] the question in what way the Freeland commonwealth guarded against the danger of *crises,* which, in my opinion, must here be much more disastrous than in any other country.

"Crises of any kind," was the answer, "would certainly dissolve the whole complex of the Freeland institutions; but here they are impossible. . . . The causes of all crises, whether called production-crises or capital-crises, lies simply in over-production — that is, in the disproportion between production and consumption; and this disproportion does not exist among us. . . .

266 ". . . Since our statistics always show with unerring accuracy what at the time is being produced in

every branch of industry, and since the demand as well as its influence upon prices can be exactly estimated from a careful observation of past years, therefore the revenue not only of every branch of industry, but of every separate establishment, can be beforehand so reliably calculated that nothing short of natural catastrophes can cause errors worth notice. If such occur, then comes in the assistance of the reciprocal insurance. . . .”

267   “And do not foreign crises sometimes disturb the calm course of your Freeland production? Are not your markets flooded, through foreign over-production, with goods for which there is no corresponding demand?” I asked.

    “It certainly cannot be denied that we are considerably inconvenienced by the frequent and sudden changes of price in the markets of the world caused by the anarchic character of the exploiting system of production. We are thereby often compelled to diminish our production in certain directions, and divert the labour thus set free to other branches of indus-
268 try. . . . We import only those goods which we cannot produce so cheaply ourselves. . . .[T]he imported goods are not presented to us, but must be paid for by the goods produced by us, [so] it is of importance that we should be able to produce the goods with which we make the payment more cheaply — that is, with less expenditure of labour-power — than we could the imported goods. . . .”

275   “. . . Among us, on the contrary, [replied Mr. Ney] everyone is alike interested in the gains of profitable investments in proportion to the amount of work he does; and everyone is also called upon to contribute to the defraying of the cost in proportion to the amount
276 of work he does: hence, a conflict/of interests, or even a mere disproportion in reaping the advantage, is among us excluded. . . . Therefore, with perfect confidence, we commit the decision of such questions to those who are most immediately interested in them. They know best what will be of advantage to them, and as their advantage is everybody's advantage, so everybody's — that is, the commonwealth's — treasury stands as open and free to them as their own. If they wish to put their hands into it, the deeper the better! We have not to inquire *whom* the investment will benefit, but merely *if* it is profitable — that is, if it saves labour.” . . .

277   “. . . What prompts your producers to run risks — small though they may be — when the profit to be gained thereby must so quickly be shared by everybody?”

    “In the first place,” replied Mr. Ney, “you overlook the fact that the amount of the expected profit is not the only inducement by which working-men, and particularly our Freeland workers, are influenced. The ambition of seeing the establishment to which one belongs in the van and not in the rear of all others, is not to be undervalued as a motive actuating intelligent men possessing a strong *esprit de corps*. But, apart from that, you must reflect that the members of the associations have also a very considerable *material* interest in the prosperity of their own particular undertaking. Freeland workers without exception have very comfortable,/nay, luxurious homes, naturally for the 278 most part in the neighborhood of their respective workplaces; they run a risk of having to leave these homes if their undertaking is not kept up to a level with others. In the second place, the elder workmen — that is, those that have been engaged a longer time in an undertaking — enjoy a constantly increasing premium; their work-time has a higher value by several units per cent. than that of the later comers. Hence, notwithstanding the solidarity of interest, the members of each association have to take care that their establishment is not excelled. . . . The associations zealously compete with each other for pre-eminence, only it is a friendly rivalry and not a competitive struggle for bread.” . . .

    . . . Here everybody enjoys sound secondary edu- 281 cation; and that a young man becomes an artisan and not a teacher, or a physician, or engineer, or such like, is due to the fact that he does not possess, or thinks he does not possess, any *exceptional* intellectual capacity. For in this country the intellectual professions can be successfully carried on only by those who possess exceptional natural qualifications, since the competition of *all* who are really qualified makes it impossible for the imperfectly qualified to succeed. . . . [I]n Freeland manual labour does not degrade. . . . 282 The common level of culture is so high, interest in the most exalted problems of humanity so general, even among the manual labourers, that *savants,* artists, heads of the government, find innumerable points of contact, both intellectual and aesthetic, even with factory-hands and agricultural labourers.

    This is all the more the case since a definite line of demarcation between head-workers and hand-workers cannot here be drawn. The manual labourer of to-day may to-morrow, by the choice of his fellow-labourers, become a director of labour, therefore a head-worker. . . ./[T]here is a still larger number of 283 persons who combine some kind of manual labour with intellectual work. . . .[I]n all the higher callings, and even in the public offices, arrangements have to be made which will allow those engaged in such offices. . . . to demand, besides the regular two months' holiday, leave of absence for a longer or a shorter time, which time is to be spent in some other occupation. Naturally no wages are paid for the time consumed by these special periods of absence; but this does not prevent the greater part of all these officials from seeking a temporary change of occupation for several months once in every two or three years, as factory-hands, miners, agriculturists, gardeners, &c. . . .

In view of this general and thorough inter-blending of the most ordinary physical with the highest mental activity, it is impossible to speak of any distinction of class or social status. . . .

But the women . . . in this country are the most zealous advocates of a complete amalgamation of all the different sections of the population. The Freeland 284 woman, almost without exception, has/attained to a very high degree of ethical and intellectual culture. Relieved of all material anxiety and toil, her sole vocation is to ennoble herself, to quicken her understanding for all that is good and lofty. . . .

The women here . . . are free and endowed with equal legal rights with the men in the highest sense of the words. . . .

. . . . .

289   . . . "But it appears to me . . . remarkable that your principle of granting a right of maintenance to all who are incapable of working, whatever may be the occasion of that incapacity, has not overwhelmed you with invalids and old people without number. Or have we yet to learn of some provisions made to defend you from such guests? . . ."

"No distinction is made with respect to the right to a maintenance-allowance, a sufficient qualification for which is a certificate of illness signed by one of our public physicians, or proof of having attained to the age of sixty years. The greatest liberality is exercised on principle in granting the medical certificate; indeed, everyone has the right, if one physician has refused to grant a certificate, to go to any other physician, as we prefer to support ten lazy impostors rather than reject one real invalid. . . . In this matter also, the influence of our institutions is found to be powerful enough to nip all such tendencies in the bud. Note, above all, that the strongest ambition of the immigrant is to become like us, to become incorporated with us; in order to this, if he is healthy and strong, he must participate in our affairs. . . .

290   "From the founding of our commonwealth we have insisted upon the ability to read and write sufficiently to be able to participate in all our rights. . . ."

291   "Then," said my father, "your boasted equality of rights exists only for educated persons?"

"Of course," explained Mrs. Ney. "Or do you really believe that perfectly uneducated persons possess the power of disciplining themselves? Certainly, real freedom and equality of rights presuppose some degree of culture. . . .[W]ealth and leisure are the products of higher art and culture, and can be possessed only by truly civilised men. . . ."

"I must ask you to remove yet one other difficul- 292 ty, and one that seems to me to be the greatest of all. What of the criminals, against whose immigration you are not protected? To me it seems most strange that, with the millions of your Freeland population, you can dispense with both police and penal code. . . . Have your institutions such a strong ameliorating power over hardened criminals?"

"Certainly," answered Mrs. Ney. "And if you carefully consider what is the essential and ultimate source of all crime, you will find/this is quite intelli- 293 gible. . . ./In economic matters we require of the indi- 294 vidual nothing that is antagonistic to his interests; it follows as a matter of course that he never rebels against our laws. . . .

"But you ask, further, how does it happen that those unfortunates who in other countries are driven into crime, not by want, but by their evil disposition . . . do not give us any trouble? . . . This hatred towards society and its members is not natural, is not innate in even the worst of men, but is the product of the injustice in the midst of which habitual criminals live. . . . /We have a few dozen incorrigibly vicious persons in 295 the country, but these are without exception incurable idiots. . . .[A]s soon as their mental unsoundness was ascertained, they were placed in asylums." . . .

". . . We have demonstrated that civilisation is 297 not merely compatible with, but is necessarily implied in, the economic equality of rights. . . ."

"Then you think," I said, "that equality of actual income has nothing to do with equality *of rights*? . . ."

". . . Among us inequality exists only so far as 299 the difference of capacity justifies it; and we have seen that, in proportion as wealth increases, the distribution of it becomes automatically more and more equal. As in this country everything is controlled by a competition which is free in fact, and not in name merely, it follows as a necessary result that every kind of capacity is better paid the rarer it is. . . . Only when superior intellectual gifts are connected with knowledge and experience in business can the man who performs headwork expect to obtain higher pay than the manual labourer. Yet even here there is to be seen a *relative* diminution of the higher pay. In the early years of Freeland a specially talented leader of production could demand six times as much as the average earnings of a labourer; at present three times as much as the average is a rare maximum, which in the domain of material production is exceeded only in isolated cases of preeminent inventors. On the other hand, the earnings of gifted authors and artists in this country have no definite limits; as their works are above competition, so the rewards they obtain bear no proportion to those obtainable in ordinary business.

"But in this way, I think, the most delicate sense of equality can be satisfied. Economic equality of rights never produces absolute and universal equality. . . ."

. . . . .

304   . . . Mr. Ney explained to us that in Freeland the reciprocal declaration of two lovers that they wished to become husband and wife was all that was required to the conclusion of a marriage-contract. The young people had nothing further to do than to make such an express declaration, and they would be married.

"Of course the marriage-contract is communicated to the Statistical Department as quickly as possible, but this enrolment has nothing to do with the validity of the contract; and as to the protection of the marriage-bond, we know of no other here than that which is to be found in the reciprocal affection of the married pair," said Mrs. Ney.

305   "If you take a comprehensive view of the whole complex of our economic and social institutions," said she [Mrs Ney] to my father, "you will see why in Freeland man and wife must regard each other with different eyes than is the case in Europe or America. . . . That well-to-do intelligent men do not steal and rob, that in a highly cultivated society which guarantees to everyone the undiminished product of his own labour no one touches the fruits of another man's industry — this is not more self-evident than it is that the same principle of economic justice must smother in the germ all longing for the wife or the husband of another. . . . Sexual honour and fidelity, like honesty in matters of property, are rare "virtues" only where they impose upon the individual the exercise of a self-denial which is not reconcilable with the instinct of self-preservation; where, as among us, a harmony of interests is established even in this domain, where everyone gets the whole of what is his own, and no one is expected to forego in the common interest of the community what belongs to himself — here even this virtue is transformed into a rational self-interest which every accountable person exhibits spontaneously and without any compulsion from without, as something

306 that he owes to himself. We are all/faithful because faithfulness does not impose upon any one of us the renunciation of his individuality." . . .

. . . . .

442 The history of "Freeland" is ended. I could go on with the thread of the narrative, and depict the work of

human emancipation as it appears to my mental eye, but of what use would it be? Those who have not been convinced, by what I have already written, that we are standing on the threshold of a new and happier age, and that it depends solely upon our discernment and resolve whether we pass over it, would not be convinced by a dozen volumes.

For this book is not the idle creation of an uncontrolled imagination, but the outcome of earnest, sober reflection, and of profound and scientific investigation. All that I have described as really happening *might* happen if men were found who, convinced as I am of the untenability of existing conditions, determined to act instead of merely complaining. . . .

It will perhaps be objected, "Thus have numberless reformers spoken and written, since the days of Sir Thomas More; and what has been proposed to mankind as a panacea for all suffering has always proved to be Utopian." . . ./The reader who does not 443 for himself discover the difference between this book and the works of imagination above referred to, is lost to me. . . .

The impartial reader, on the other hand, will not be prevented by the narrative form of this book from soberly endeavouring to discover whether my propositions are essentially true or false. If he should find that I have started from false premises, that the system of freedom and justice which I have propounded is inconsistent in any way with the natural and universally recognised springs of human action — nay, if, after reading my book, he should not have attained to the firm conviction that the realisation of this new order — apart, of course, from unimportant details — is absolutely inevitable, then I must be content to be placed in the same category as More, Fourier, Cabet, and the rest who have mistaken their desires for sober reality.

TOPICS FOR SHORT PAPERS

The rationale for Freeland
The reasons behind the writing of *Looking Backward* and *Freeland*
The significance of "Freeland" as a name for the new nation
Suffrage in Freeland

EXERCISE

Read these passages carefully; then follow the directions on page 41.
[*The following conversation takes place among Prince Falieri, Carlo, and Mrs. Ney shortly after the Falieris arrived in Freeland.*]
"With such a universal taste for the beautiful among 211

your people," said my father to Mrs. Ney, "I am surprised that so little attention is given to the adornment of the most beautiful embellishment of Freeland — its queenly women. . . . [O]f actual ornaments one sees none at all. Here and there a gold fastener in the hair, here and there a gold or silver brooch on the dress — that is all; precious stones and pearls seem to be avoided by the ladies here. What is the reason for this?"

"The reason is," answered Mrs. Ney, "that the sole motive which makes ornaments so sought after among other nations is absent from us in Freeland. Vanity is native here also, among both men and women; but it does not find any satisfaction in the display of so-called 'valuables,' things whose only superiority consists in their being dear. Do you really believe that it is the *beauty* of the diamond which leads so many of our pitiable sisters in other parts of the world to stake happiness and honour in order to get possession of such glittering little bits of stone? Why does the woman who has sold herself for a genuine stone thrust aside as unworthy of notice the imitation stone which in reality she cannot distinguish from the real one? And do you doubt that the real diamond would itself be degraded to the rank of a valueless piece of crystal which no 'lady of taste' would ever glance at, if it by any means lost its high price? Ornaments do not please, therefore, because they are beautiful, but because 212 they are dear. They flatter vanity not by/their brilliancy, but by giving to the owner of them the consciousness of possessing in these scarcely visible trifles the extract of so many human lives. . . .

"The power of which ornaments are the legitimate expression — the power over the lives and the bodies of others — does not exist in Freeland. Anyone possessing a diamond worth, for example, 600*l.*, would here have at his disposal a year's income from one person's labour; but to buy such a diamond and to wear it because it represented that value would, in view of our institutions, be to make oneself ridiculous; for he who did it would simply be investing in that way the profits of *his own labour.* Value for value must he give to anyone whose labour he would buy for himself with his stone; and, instead of reverent admiration, he would only excite compassion for having renounced better pleasures, or for having put forth profitless efforts, in order to acquire a paltry bit of stone. . . ."

213 "Then you do not admit that ornaments have any real adorning power? You deny that pearls or diamonds add materially to the charms of a beautiful person?" asked my father in reply.

"That I do, certainly," was the answer. "Not that I dispute their decorative effect altogether; only I assert that they do not produce the same and, as a rule, not so good an effect as can be produced by other means. . . . That in other parts of the world a lady decked with diamonds pleases you gentlemen better than one decked with

flowers is due to the same cause that makes you — though you may be staunch Republicans — see more beauty in a queen than in her rivals. . . . Let the rose become the symbol of authority to be worn only by queens, and you would without any doubt find that roses were the adornment best fitted to reveal true majesty."

"But the precious metals" — thus I interposed — "are not so completely abjured in Freeland as precious stones and pearls. Is there no inconsistency here?"

"I think not," answered Mrs. Ney. "We make use of any material in proportion to its beauty and suitability. If we find gems or pearls really useful for decorative purposes, and sufficiently beautiful when thus used to compensate in their aesthetic attractiveness for their cost, we make use of them without hesitation. But that does not apply to jewels as personal ornaments: the natural rose is, under all circumstances, a better adornment than its imitation in rubies and diamonds. The precious metals, on the other hand, have certain properties — durability, lustre, and extraordinary malleability — which in many cases make it imperative to employ them for decorative purposes. Nevertheless, even their employment is very limited among us. . . ./In short, we use the noble metals never 214 *because* of, but now and then *in spite of,* their costliness."

. . . . .

[The director of the Freeland Bank explains the basis of Freeland's monetary system to the Falieris and other visitors.]

". . . Now, among us in Freeland *all* labour-power is 246 as well equipped and applied as possible, because the perfect and unlimited freedom of labour to apply itself at any time to whatever will create the highest value brings about, if not/an absolute, yet a relative equilibrium of 247 values; but, in order that this may be brought about, there must exist an unchangeable and reliable standard by which the value of the things produced by labour can be measured. . . . Consequently we, more imperatively than any other people, need a measure of value as accurate and reliable as possible — that is, one the exchange-power of which, with reference to all other things, is exposed to as little variation as possible. This best possible, most constant, standard the civilised world has hitherto found rightly in gold. There is no difference in value between two equal quantities of gold, whilst one labour-day may be very materially more valuable than another; and there is no means of ascertaining with certainty the difference in value of the two labour-days except by comparing them both with one and the same thing which possesses a really constant value. Yet this equality in value in equal quantities of gold is the least of the advantages possessed by gold over other measures of value. Two equal quantities of wheat are of nearly/equal value. But the value of gold 248 is exposed to less *variation* than is the value of any other thing. . . . If its exchange-relation to any commodity whatever alters suddenly and considerably, it can be at once and with certainty assumed that it is the value not of the gold, but of the other commodity, which has sud-

Theodor Hertzka, *Freeland.* New York: D. Appleton and Co., 1891.

denly and considerably altered. . . . This, then, is the reason why gold is the best possible, though by no means an absolutely perfect, measure of value. But labour-time would be the worst conceivable measure of value, for neither are two equal periods of labour necessarily of equal value, nor does labour-time in general possess an unalterable value, but its exchange-power in relation to all other things increases with every step forward in the methods of labour."

A. Take quotation and critical notes on the above passages. Use three-by-five note cards unless your instructor directs otherwise.

B. All of the questions asked in Exercise A, page 16, are also pertinent to the Freelanders' concept of the usefulness and worth of precious metals and gems. Answer each of the following questions in a single statement which could serve as the *thesis sentence* for a short paper.
According to the Freelanders' view, what is the natural value of precious metal and gems?
According to their view, why are precious metals and gems held in esteem in other societies?
How are precious metals and gems used in Freeland?
Why are they found useful in Freeland?

C. In writing a research paper from printed sources, you will occasionally discover new evidence or material after you have begun to write. Considering Hertzka's ideas on precious metals and gems in this light, revise the paper you wrote for Exercise B, page 16, by incorporating statements and concepts from *Freeland*. Begin by revising and restating your thesis sentence if necessary. Be sure to footnote the material from *Freeland*.

A SELECTED BIBLIOGRAPHY

"The Freeland Colony Scheme," *All the Year Round,* LXXV (1894), 65-69.

The Gentlemen's Magazine, CCLXXII (1892), 108. [A review]

Gümpel, C. Godfrey. "A Possible Solution of the Social Question," *Westminster Review,* CXXXVIII (1892), 270-285.

Hertzka, Theodor. *Eine Reise nach Freiland.* Leipzig, 1893. [A continuation of *Freeland;* never translated into English]

Jenks, Jeremiah W. *Political Science Quarterly,* V (1890), 706-708. [A review]

Knödel, Karl. "Side-Lights on Socialism," *The Fortnightly Review,* LXIII (1895), 250-276.

Magazine of American History, XXVIII (1892), 78. [A review]

The Nation, L (1890), 32-34. [A review]

Westminster Review, CXXXVI (1891), 442-443. [A review] . .

SUBJECTS FOR LIBRARY PAPERS

The influence of Auguste Comte on the organization of Freeland's social institutions
The failure of the Freeland colony
Freeland's associations and more recent communes and community farms

MORRIS: News From Nowhere

William Morris. NEWS FROM NOWHERE, Vol. XVI of THE COLLECTED WORKS OF WILLIAM MORRIS, with Introduction by His Daughter May Morris. 24 vols. London: Longmans, Green & Co., 1910–1915.

Artist, artisan, poet, printer, socialist, William Morris (1834-1896) wrote News from Nowhere *in 1891. Disgusted by the ugliness as well as by the inequality of industrialized Victorian England, Morris synthesizes his aesthetic and political ideals in this work.*

William Guest falls asleep in the grimy England of the 1880's and dreams that he awakens at some unspecified future date when England is again green and beautiful. Emerging from the Guest House in which he has awakened, Guest meets Dick, who offers to guide him through this new world. Guest accepts the offer, and the two set off immediately for London. On the way Guest sees a group of children playing in the woods.

28   "Well, the youngsters here will be all the fresher for school when the summer gets over and they have to go back again."

"School?" he said; "yes, what do you mean by that word? . . ."

. . . "I was using the word in the sense of a 29 system of education,/. . . a system of teaching young people."

"Why not old people also?" said he with a twinkle in his eye. "But," he went on, "I can assure you our children learn, whether they go through a 'system of teaching' or not. Why, you will not find one of these children about here, boy or girl, who cannot swim; and every one of them has been used to tumbling about the little forest ponies. . . . They all of them know how to cook; the bigger lads can mow; many can thatch and do odd jobs at carpentering; or they know how to keep shop. I can tell you they know plenty of things."

"Yes, but their mental education, the teaching of their minds," said I, kindly translating my phrase.

"Guest," said he, "perhaps you have not learned to do these things I have been speaking about; and if that's the case, don't you run away with the idea that it doesn't take some skill to do them, and doesn't give plenty of work for one's mind. . . . But, however, I understand you to be speaking of book-learning; and as to that, it is a simple affair. Most children, seeing books lying about, manage to read by the time they are four years old. . . . As to writing, we do not encourage them to scrawl too early . . . because it gets them into a habit of ugly writing; and what's the use of a lot of ugly writing being done, when rough printing can be done so easily. . . ."

"Well," said I, "about the children; when they 30 know how to read and write, don't they learn something else — languages, for instance?"

"Of course," he said; "sometimes even before they can read, they can talk French . . . and they soon get to know German also. . . . These are the principal languages we speak in these islands, along with English or Welsh, or Irish, which is another form of Welsh; and children pick them up very quickly, because their elders all know them; and besides our guests from over sea often bring their children with them, and the little ones get together, and rub their speech into one another."

"And the older languages?" said I.

"O, yes," said he, "they mostly learn Latin and Greek along with the modern ones, when they do anything more than merely pick up the latter."

"And history?" said I; "how do you teach history?"

"Well," said he, "when a person can read, of course he reads what he likes to; and he can easily get someone to tell him what are the best books to read on such or such a subject, or to explain what he doesn't understand in the books when he is reading them."

"Well," said I, "what else do they learn? I suppose they don't all learn history?"

"No, no," said he; "some don't care about it; in fact, I don't think many do. . . . No; many people study facts about the make of things and the matters of cause and effect, so that knowledge increases on us, if that be good; and some . . . will spend time over mathematics. 'Tis no use forcing people's tastes."

31 Said I: "But you don't mean that children learn all these things?"

Said he: "That depends on what you mean by children; and also you must remember how much they differ. As a rule, they don't do much reading, except for a few story-books, till they are about fifteen years old; we don't encourage early bookishness: though you will find some children who *will* take to books very early; which perhaps is not good for them; but it's no use thwarting them. . . . You see, children are mostly given to imitating their elders, and when they see most people about them engaged in genuinely amusing work, like house-building and street-paving, and gardening, and the like, that is what they want to be doing; so I don't think we need fear having too many book-learned men." . . .

But my companion couldn't quite let his subject drop, and went on meditatively:

"After all, I don't know that it does them much harm, even if they do grow up book-students. Such people as that, 'tis a great pleasure seeing them so happy over work which is not much sought for. And besides, these students are generally such pleasant people, so kind and sweet tempered; so humble, and at the same time so anxious to teach everybody all that they know. . . ."

32 We went on a little further, and I looked to the right again, and said, in a rather doubtful tone of voice, "Why, there are the Houses of Parliament! Do you still use them?"

He burst out laughing, and was some time before he could control himself; then he clapped me on the back and said:

"I take you, neighbour; you may well wonder at our keeping them standing, and I know something about that, and my old kinsman has given me books to read about the strange game that they played there. Use them! Well, yes, they are used for a sort of subsidiary market, and a storage place for manure. . . ."

[As the ride continues, the conversation turns to two other aspects of life in this new England.]

44 Quoth I: "But have you no prisons at all now?"

As soon as the words were out of my mouth, I felt that I had made a mistake, for Dick flushed red and frowned. . . .

"Man alive! how can you ask such a question? Have I not told you that we know what a prison means by the undoubted evidence of really trustworthy books, helped out by our own imaginations? And haven't you specially called me to notice that the people about the roads and streets look happy? and how could they look happy if they knew that their neighbours were shut up in prison, while they bore such things quietly? . . . Prisons, indeed! O no, no, no!"

. . . . .

. . . "What building is that?" said I, eagerly. . . . 46 "[I]t seems to be a factory."

"Yes," he said, "I think I know what you mean, and that's what it is; but we don't call them factories now, but Banded-workshops: that is, places where people collect who want to work together."

"I suppose," said I, "power of some sort is used there?"

"No, no," said he. "Why should people collect together to use power, when they can have it at the places where they live, or hard by, any two or three of them; or any one, for the matter of that? No; folk collect in these Banded-workshops to do hand-work in which working together is necessary or convenient; such work is often very pleasant. In there, for instance, they make pottery and glass. . . . Well, of course it's handy to have fair-sized ovens and kilns and glass-pots, and a good lot of things to use them for: though of course there are a good many such places, as it would be ridiculous if a man had a liking for pot-making or glass-blowing that he should have to live in one place or be obliged to forego the work he liked."

. . . . .

[Guest and Dick arrive at the home of old Hammond, who is willing to answer Guest's many questions about the country in which he has awakened. There they also meet Clara, and Guest's first question concerns Clara and Dick.]

Said I: "That beautiful girl, is he going to be 55 married to her?"

"Well," said he, "yes, he is. He has been married to her once already, and now I should say it is pretty clear that he will be married to her again."

"Indeed," quoth I, wondering what that meant.

"Here is the whole tale," said old Hammond. . . . "[T]hey lived together two years the first time; were both very young; and then she got it into her head that she was in love with somebody else. So she left poor Dick; I say *poor* Dick, because he had not found anyone else. . . ."

56 "Dear me," said I. "Have they any children?"

"Yes," said he, "two; they are staying with one of my daughters at present, where, indeed, Clara has mostly been. I wouldn't lose sight of her, as I felt sure they would come together again. . . . So I managed it all; as I have done with such-like matters before."

"Ah," said I, "no doubt you wanted to keep them out of the Divorce Court: but I suppose it often has to settle such matters."

"Then you suppose nonsense," said he. "I know that there used to be such lunatic affairs as divorce-courts: but just consider; all the cases that came into them were matters of property quarrels: and I think, dear guest . . . you can see from the mere outside look of our world that quarrels about private property could not go on amongst us in our days." . . .

Well, then, property quarrels being no longer possible, what remains in these matters that a court of law could deal with? Fancy a court for enforcing a contract of passion or sentiment! If such a thing were needed as a *reductio ad absurdum* of the enforcement of contract, such a folly would do that for us."

He was silent again a little, and then said: ". . ./ 57 We do not deceive ourselves, indeed, or believe that we can get rid of all the trouble that besets the dealings between the sexes. We know that we must face the unhappiness that comes of man and woman confusing the relations between natural passion, and sentiment, and the friendship which, when things go well, softens the awakening from passing illusions: but we are not so mad as to pile up degradation on that unhappiness by engaging in sordid squabbles about livelihood and position, and the power of tyrannising over the children who have been the results of love or lust,"

59 ". . . Now may I ask you about the position of women in your society?" . . .

"Well," said he, ". . . The men have no longer any opportunity of tyrannising over the women, or the women over the men. . . . The women do what they can do best, and what they like best, and the men are neither jealous of it or injured by it. . . ."

60 "Very well," I said; "but about this woman question? I saw at the Guest House that the women were waiting on the men: that seems a little like reaction, doesn't it?"

"Does it?" said the old man; "perhaps you think housekeeping an unimportant occupation, not deserving of respect. . . . [D]on't you know that it is a great pleasure to a clever woman to manage a house skillfully, and to do it so that all the house-mates about

her look pleased, and are grateful to her? . . ./ [Fur- 61 thermore] [h]ow could it possibly be but that maternity should be highly honoured amongst us? . . . For the rest, remember that all the *artificial* burdens of motherhood are now done away with. A mother has no longer any mere sordid anxieties for the future of her children. They may indeed turn out better or worse; they may disappoint her highest hopes; such anxieties as these are a part of the mingled pleasure and pain which goes to make up the life of mankind. But at least she is spared the fear . . . that artificial disabilities would make her children something less than men and women: she knows that they will live and act according to the measure of/their own faculties. . . ." 62

. . . . .

Said I: "I want an extra word or two about your 63 ideas of education; although I gathered from Dick that you let your children run wild and didn't teach them anything. . . ."

"Then you gathered left-handed," quoth he. . . . "But, however, to put it in a cooler way: you expected to see children thrust into schools when they had reached an age conventionally supposed to be the due age, whatever their varying faculties and dispositions might be, and when there, with like disregard to/facts 64 to be subjected to a certain conventional course of 'learning.' My friend, can't you see that such a proceeding means ignoring the fact of *growth*, bodily and mental? No one could come out of such a mill uninjured; and those only would avoid being crushed by it who would have the spirit of rebellion strong in them. . . . All that is past; we are no longer hurried, and the information lies ready to each one's hand when his own inclinations impel him to seek it. In this as in other matters we have become wealthy: we can afford to give ourselves time to grow." . . .

"Now," said I, "I have come to the point of ask- 75 ing questions which I suppose will be dry for you to answer and difficult for you to explain; but I have foreseen for some time past that I must ask them. . . . What kind of government have you? . . ."

". . . I must now shock you by telling you that we have no longer anything which you . . . would call a government."

"I am not so much shocked as you might think. . . . But tell me, how do you manage, and how have you come to this state of things?"

Said he: "It is true that we have to make some arrangements about our affairs, concerning which you can ask presently; and it is also true that everybody does not always agree with the details of these arrangements; but, further, it is true that a man no more needs an elaborate system of government, with its army, navy, and police, to force him to give way to the will of the majority of his *equals,* than he wants a similar machinery to make him understand that his head and a stone/wall cannot occupy the same space at the same moment. . . ."

79 "Well," I said, "about those 'arrangements' which you spoke of as taking the place of government, could you give me any account of them?"

". . . I can better tell you what we don't do, than what we do do."

80 "Well?" said I.

"This is the way to put it," said he: "We have been living for a hundred and fifty years, at least, more or less in our present manner, and a tradition or habit of life has been growing on us; and that habit has become a habit of acting on the whole for the best. It is easy for us to live without robbing each other. It would be possible for us to contend with and rob each other, but it would be harder for us than refraining from strife and robbery. That is in short the foundation of our life and our happiness." . . .

"But as to these days," I said; "you don't mean to tell me that no one ever transgresses this habit of good fellowship?"

"Certainly not," said Hammond, "but when the transgressions occur, everybody, transgressors and all, know them for what they are; the errors of friends, not the habitual actions of persons driven into enmity against society."

"I see," said I; "you mean that you have no 'criminal' classes."

"How could we have them," said he, "since there is no rich class to breed enemies against the state by means of the injustice of the state?"

Said I: "I thought that I understood from something that fell from you a little while ago that you had abolished civil law. Is that so, literally?"

"It abolished itself, my friend," said he. "As I said before, the civil law-courts were upheld for the defence of private property; for nobody ever pretended that it was possible to make people act fairly to each other by means of brute force. Well, private property 81 being abolished, all the laws and all/the legal 'crimes' which it had manufactured of course came to an end. Thou shalt not steal, had to be translated into, Thou shalt work in order to live happily. . . ."

"Well," said I, ". . . how about the crimes of violence? would not their occurrence (and you admit that they occur) make criminal law necessary?"

Said he: "In your sense of the word, we have no criminal law either. . . . By far the greater part of these [crimes] in past days were the result of the laws of private property. . . . All *that* cause of violent crime is gone. Again, many violent acts came from the artificial perversion of the sexual passions, which caused overweening jealousy and like miseries. Now, when you look carefully into these, you will find that what lay at the bottom of them was mostly the idea (a law-made idea) of the woman being the property of the man. . . . *That* idea has of course vanished with private property. . . .

"Another cognate cause of crimes of violence was the family tyranny. . . . Of course that is all ended, since families are held together by no bond of coercion, legal or social, but by mutual liking and affection, and everybody is free to come or go as he or she pleases. . . ."

"Yes," I said, "but consider, must not the safety 82 of society be safeguarded by some punishment?"

". . . [W]e who live amongst our friends need neither fear nor punish. Surely if we, in dread of an occasional rare homicide, an occasional rough blow, were solemnly and legally to commit homicide and violence, we could only be a society of ferocious cowards. . . . Yet you must understand . . . that when any violence is committed, we expect the transgressor to make any atonement possible to him, and he himself expects it. But again, think if the destruction or serious/injury of 83 a man momentarily overcome by wrath or folly can be any atonement to the commonwealth? Surely it can only be an additional injury to it."

Said I: "But suppose the man has a habit of violence, — kills a man a year, for instance?"

"Such a thing is unknown," said he. "In a society where there is no punishment to evade, no law to triumph over, remorse will certainly follow transgression."

"And lesser outbreaks of violence," said I, "how do you deal with them? . . ."

Said Hammond: "If the ill-doer is not sick or mad (in which case he must be restrained till his sickness or madness is cured) it is clear that grief and humiliation must follow the ill-deed; and society in general will make that pretty clear to the ill-doer if he should chance to be dull to it; and again, some kind of atonement will follow, — at the least, an open acknowledgment of the grief and humiliation. Is it so hard to say, I ask your pardon, neighbour? — Well, sometimes it is hard — and let it be." . . .

"So," said I, "you consider crime a mere spasmodic disease, which requires no body of criminal law to deal with it?"

"Pretty much so," said he; "and since, as I have told you, we are a healthy people generally, so we are not likely to be much troubled with *this* disease." . . .

Said I: "How do you manage with politics?" 85

Said Hammond, smiling: ". . . I will answer your question briefly by saying that we are very well off as to politics, — because we have none. . . ."

Said I: "How about your relations with foreign nations?"

". . . [T]he whole system of rival and contending nations which played so great a part in the 'government' of the world of civilisation has disappeared along with the inequality betwixt man and man in society. 86 . . ./[W]e are all bent on the same enterprise, making the most of our lives. And I must tell you whatever quarrels or misunderstandings arise, they very seldom take place between people of different race; and consequently since there is less unreason in them, they are the more readily appeased."

"Good," said I, "but as to those matters of politics; as to general differences of opinion in one and the same community. Do you assert that there are none?"

"No, not at all," said he, somewhat snappishly; "but I do say that differences of opinion about real solid things need not, and with us do not, crystallise people into parties permanently hostile to one another. . . ."

87 Said I: "And you settle these differences, great and small, by the will of the majority, I suppose?"

"Certainly," said he; "how else could we settle them? You see in matters which are merely personal which do not affect the welfare of the community — how a man shall dress, what he shall eat and drink, what he shall write and read, and so forth — there can be no difference of opinion, and everybody does as he pleases. But when the matter is of common interest to the whole community, and the doing or not doing something affects everybody, the majority must have their way; unless the minority were to take up arms and show by force that they were the effective or real majority; which, however, in a society of men who are free and equal is little likely to happen; because in such a community the apparent majority *is* the real majority, and the others, as I have hinted before, know that too well to obstruct from mere pigheadedness; especially as they have had plenty of opportunity of putting forward their side of the question."

"How is that managed?" said I.

88 "Well," said he, "let us take one of our units of management. . . . In such a district, as you would call it, some neighbours think that something ought to be done or undone. . . . Well, at the next ordinary meeting of the neighbours, or Mote, . . . a neighbour proposes the change, and of course, if everybody agrees, there is an end of discussion, except about details. Equally, if no one backs the proposer, . . . the matter drops for the time being. . . . But supposing the affair proposed and seconded, if a few of the neighbours dis-

agree to it . . . they don't count heads that time, but put off the formal discussion to the next Mote; and meantime arguments *pro* and *con* are flying about, and some get printed, so that everybody knows what is going on; and when the Mote comes together again there is a regular discussion and at last a vote by show of hands. If the division is a close one, the question is again put off for further discussion; if the division is a wide one, the minority are asked if they will yield to the more general opinion, which they often, nay, most commonly do. If they refuse, the question is debated a third time, when, if the minority has not perceptibly grown, they always give way. . . ."

"Very good," said I; "but what happens if the 89 divisions are still narrow?"

Said he: "As a matter of principle and according to the rule of such cases, the question must then lapse, and the majority, if so narrow, has to submit to sitting down under the *status quo*. But I must tell you that in point of fact the minority very seldom enforces this rule, but generally yields in a friendly manner. . . . The only alternatives to our method that I can conceive of are these. First, that we should choose out, or breed, a class of superior persons capable of judging on all matters without consulting the neighbours. . . . Secondly, that for the purpose of safe-guarding the freedom of the individual will, we should revert to a system of private property again, and have slaves and slave-holders once more. . . ."

"Well," said I, "there is a third possibility — to wit, that every man should be quite independent of every other, and that thus the tyranny of society should be abolished."

He looked hard at me for a second or two, and then burst out laughing very heartily; and I confess that I joined him. When he recovered himself he nodded at me, and said: "Yes, yes, I quite agree with you — and so we all do."

. . . . .

". . . Now, this is what I want to ask you about 91 — to wit, how you get people to work when there is no reward of labour, and especially how you get them to work strenuously?"

"No reward of labour?" said Hammond, gravely. . . . Plenty of reward . . . the reward of creation. . . . [W]hereas we are not short of wealth, there is a kind of/fear growing up amongst us that we shall one 92 day be short of work. It is a pleasure which we are afraid of losing, not a pain. . . . [A]ll work is now pleasurable; either because of the hope of gain in honour and wealth with which the work is done, which causes pleasurable excitement, even when the actual work is not pleasant; or else because it has grown into a pleasurable *habit*, as in the case with what you may call mechanical work; and lastly (and most of our work is of this kind) because there is conscious sensuous pleasure in the work itself; it is done, that is, by artists."

"I see," said I. "Can you now tell me how you have come to this happy condition? . . ."

"Briefly," said he, "by the absence of artificial coercion, and the freedom for every man to do what he can do best, joined to the knowledge of what productions of labour we really want. . . ."

. . . . .

97   . . . "The wares which we make are made because they are needed: men make for their neighbours' use as if they were making for themselves, not for a vague market of which they know nothing, and over which they have no control: as there is no buying and selling, it would be mere insanity to make goods on the chance of their being wanted; for there is no longer anyone who can be *compelled* to buy them. So that whatever is made is good, and thoroughly fit for its purpose. Nothing *can* be made except for genuine use; therefore no inferior goods are made. Moreover . . . we have now found out what we want, so we make no more than we want; and as we are not driven to make a vast quantity of useless things, we have time and resources enough to consider our pleasure in making them. All work which would be irksome to do by hand is done by immensely improved machinery; and in all work which it is a pleasure to do by hand machinery is done without. There is no difficulty in finding work which suits the special turn of mind of everybody; so that no man is sacrificed to the wants of another. From time to time, when we have found that some piece of work was too disagreeable or troublesome, we have given it up and done altogether without the thing produced by it. Now, surely you can see that under these circumstances all the work that we do is an exercise of the mind and body more or less pleasant to be done: so that instead of avoiding work everybody seeks it. . . ."

[*"Meantime, my friend," Hammond tells Guest at one point in their conversation, "you must know that we are too happy, both individually and collectively, to trouble ourselves about what is to come hereafter." After describing the bloody revolution which was necessary before this happy state could be established, Hammond discusses the religion of the new state more fully.*]

132   ". . . The spirit of the new days, of our days, was to be delight in the life of the world; intense and overweening love of the very skin and surface of the earth on which man dwells, such as a lover has in the fair flesh of the woman he loves; this, I say, was to be the new spirit of the time. . . . [A]nd now we do, both in word and in deed, believe in the continuous life of the world of men, and as it were, add every day of that common life to the little stock of days which our own mere individual experience wins for us: and consequently we are happy. . . ./[W]here is the difficulty in   133 accepting the religion of humanity, when the men and women who go to make up humanity are free, happy, and energetic at least, and most commonly beautiful of body also, and surrounded by beautiful things of their own fashioning, and a nature bettered and not worsened by contact with mankind? This is what this age of the world has reserved for us."

. . . . .

TOPICS FOR SHORT PAPERS

Elements of anarchy in Morris' ideal society
Crime and punishment in Morris' ideal society
The fundamental goodness of man: the foundation of the ideal societies of Bellamy and Morris
Morris' ideas about education
Morris' Utopia: progress or regression?

EXERCISE

Put the following information into the proper form for a bibliography page. Note that several items present slightly unusual problems because they contain special information about publication which must be included in the entries. Use the *MLA Style Sheet* as a guide to bibliographical form unless your instructor directs otherwise.

1. J. W. Mackail *The Life of William Morris* Longmans, Green London 1899 2 volumes
2. *William Morris, Artist, Writer, Socialist,* by May Morris With an Account of William Morris as I Knew Him, by Bernard Shaw Oxford Blackwell 2 volumes 1936
3. J. M. Murry "The Return to Fundamentals: Marx and Morris" *Adelphi* V 1932 pages 19-29, 97-109
4. "The Social Ideals of Plato and Morris" printed in *Mixed Company,* by J. C. Robertson pages 56-79 Dent London 1939
5. Tillotson, Geoffrey "Morris and Machines" Volume n.s. 135, pages 464-71 *Fortnightly Review* 1934 This essay was reprinted in Professor Tillotson's *Essays in Criticism and Research* Cambridge University Press Cambridge, England 1942 pages 144 152
6. L. W. Eshleman *A Victorian Rebel: The Life of William Morris* 1940 Scribner New York Eshleman later changed his name and the title of his book, and this same book later appeared as *William Morris, Prophet of England's New Order,* by Lloyd Eric Grey London 1949 Cassell

SUBJECTS FOR LIBRARY PAPERS

Morris as a revolutionary (Begin by reading Chapters 17 and 18 of *News from Nowhere.*)
Morris' ideas about industrialization

WELLS: A Modern Utopia

H. G. Wells. A MODERN UTOPIA. New York: Charles Scribner's Sons, 1905.

Herbert George Wells (1866-1946) wrote over eighty books: science fiction, socio-logical treatises, comedy, history, and a variety of Utopias. A Modern Utopia, written in 1904, is the first important Utopia of this century.

In the first chapter, Wells maintains that nothing less than an entire planet can serve as the location of a twentieth-century Utopia. He therefore imagines a planet, identical in its topography with that of the earth, which functions according to his idea of a proper world-state. He then goes on to describe that state and the principles on which it operates.

33 [I]n a modern Utopia . . . the State will have/
34 effectually chipped away just all those spendthrift lib-erties that waste liberty, and not one liberty more, and so have attained the maximum general freedom. . . . Prohibition takes one definite thing from the indefinite liberty of a man, but it still leaves him an unbounded choice of actions. He remains free, and you have merely taken a bucketful from the sea of his freedom. But compulsion destroys freedom altogether. In this Utopia of ours there may be many prohibitions, but no indirect compulsions . . . and few or no commands. As far as I see it now, in this present discussion, I think, indeed, there should be no positive compulsions at all in Utopia, at any rate for the adult Utopian — unless they fall upon him as penalties incurred.

. . . . .

47 The population of Utopia will be a migratory population beyond any earthly precedent, not simply a travelling population, but migratory. . . .

49 And with this loosening of the fetters of locality from the feet of men, necessarily there will be all sorts of fresh distributions of the factors of life. . . . [I]n Utopia there will be wide stretches of cheerless or un-healthy or toilsome or dangerous land with never a household; there will be regions of mining and smelt-ing, black with the smoke of furnaces and gashed and desolated by mines, with a sort of weird inhospitable grandeur of industrial desolation, and the men will

come thither and work for a spell and return to civili-zation again, washing and changing their attire in the swift gliding train. And by way of compensation there will be beautiful regions of the earth specially set apart and favoured for children; in them the presence of children will remit taxation, while in other less whole-some places the presence of children will be taxed. . . .

It is essential to the modern ideal of life that the 50 period of education and growth should be prolonged to as late a period as possible and puberty correspond-ingly retarded, and by wise regulation the statesmen of Utopia will constantly adjust and readjust regulations and taxation to diminish the proportion of children reared in hot and stimulating conditions.

. . . . .

Public drunkenness (as distinguished from the 64 mere elation that follows a generous but controlled use of wine) will be an offence against public decency, and will be dealt with in some very drastic manner. It will, of course, be an aggravation of, and not an excuse for, crime.

But I doubt whether the State will go beyond that. Whether an adult shall use wine or beer or spirits, or not, seems to me entirely a matter for his doctor and/his own private conscience. . . . The conditions of 65 physical happiness will be better understood in Utopia, it will be worth while to be well there, and the intelli-gent citizen will watch himself closely.

. . . . .

Now in the first place, a state so vast and com- 70 plex as this world Utopia, and with so migratory a people, will need some handy symbol to check the distribution of services and commodities. Almost certainly they will need to have money. . . .

77   In Utopia we conclude that, whatever other types of property may exist, all natural sources of force, and indeed all strictly natural products, coal, water power, and the like, are inalienably vested in the local authorities . . . they will generate electricity . . . and this electricity will be devoted, some of it, to the authority's lighting and other public works, some of it, as a subsidy, to the World-State authority which controls the high roads, the great railways, the inns and other apparatus of world communication, and the rest will pass on to private individuals or to distributing companies at a uniform fixed rate for private lighting and heating, for machinery and industrial applications of all sorts. Such an arrangement of affairs will necessarily involve a vast amount of book-keeping between the various authorities, the World-State government and the/cus-

78 tomers, and this book-keeping will naturally be done most conveniently in units of physical energy. . . .

      Now the problems of economic theory will have undergone an enormous clarification if, instead of measuring in fluctuating money values, the same scale of energy units can be extended to their discussion, if, in fact, the idea of trading could be entirely eliminated. . . . Every one of those giant local authorities was to be free to issue energy notes against the security of its surplus of saleable available energy, and to

79 make all/ its contracts for payment in those notes up to a certain maximum defined by the amount of energy produced and disposed of in that locality in the previous year. . . . In a world without boundaries, with a population largely migratory and emancipated from locality, the price of the energy notes of these various local bodies would constantly tend to be uniform, because employment would constantly shift into the areas where energy was cheap. Accordingly, the price of so many millions of units of energy at any particular moment in coins of the gold currency would be approximately the same throughout the world. . . . The old gold coinage was at once to cease to be legal tender beyond certain defined limits, except to the central government, which would not reissue it as it came in. It was, in fact, to become a temporary token coinage . . . and to be replaceable by an ordinary token coinage as time went on. . . .

89   The World State in this ideal presents itself as the sole landowner of the earth, with the great local governments I have adumbrated, the local municipalities, holding, as it were, feudally under it as landlords. . . . It or its tenants will produce food, and so human energy, and the exploitation of coal and electric power,

and the powers of wind and wave and water will be within its right. It will pour out this energy by assignment and lease and acquiescence and what not upon its individual citizens. It will maintain order, maintain roads, maintain a cheap and efficient administration of justice,/maintain cheap and rapid locomotion and be 90 the common carrier of the planet, convey and distribute labour, control, let, or administer all natural productions, pay for and secure healthy births and a healthy and vigorous new generation, maintain the public health, coin money and sustain standards of measurement, subsidise research, and reward such commercially unprofitable undertakings as benefit the community as a whole; subsidise when needful chairs of criticism and authors and publications, and collect and distribute information. . . . The State is for/Indi- 91 viduals, the law is for freedoms, the world is for experiment, experience, and change: these are the fundamental beliefs upon which a modern Utopia must go. . . .

      The object sought in the code of property laws 92 that one would find in operation in Utopia would be the same object that pervades the whole Utopian organisation, namely, a universal maximum of individual freedom. . . . Whatever [a man] has justly made he has a right to keep, that is obvious enough; but he will also have a right to sell and exchange, and so this question of what may be property takes really the form of what may a man buy in Utopia?

      A modern Utopian most assuredly must have a practically unqualified property in all those things that become, as it were, by possession, extensions and expressions of his personality; his clothing, his jewels, the tools of his employment, his books, the objects of art he may have bought or made, his personal weapons/(if Utopia have need of such things), insignia, 93 and so forth. All such things that he has bought with his money or acquired — provided he is not a professional or habitual dealer in such property — will be inalienably his, his to give or lend or keep, free even from taxation. So intimate is this sort of property that I have no doubt Utopia will give a man posthumous rights over it — will permit him to assign it to a successor with at the utmost the payment of a small redemption. . . . In Utopia no one will have to hunger because some love to make and have made and own and cherish beautiful/things. To give this much of 94 property to individuals will tend to make clothing, ornamentation, implements, books, and all the arts finer and more beautiful, because by buying such things a man will secure something inalienable — save in the case of bankruptcy — for himself and for those who belong to him. Moreover, a man may in his lifetime set aside sums to ensure special advantages of education and care for the immature children of himself and others, and in this manner also exercise a posthumous right.

For all other property, the Utopians will have a scantier respect; even money unspent by a man, and debts to him that bear no interest, will at his death stand upon a lower level than these things. . . . This applies, for example, to the property that a man creates and acquires in business enterprises, which are presumably undertaken for gain, and as a means of living rather than for themselves.

. . . . .

136   [Inferior] people will have to be in the descendant phase, the species must be engaged in eliminating them; there is no escape from that, and conversely the people of exceptional quality must be ascendant. The better sort of people, so far as they can be distinguished, must have the fullest freedom of public service, and the fullest opportunity of parentage. And it must be open to every man to approve himself worthy of ascendancy. . . .

138   . . . It [the State] will insist upon every citizen being properly housed, well nourished, and in good health, reasonably clean and clothed healthily, and upon that insistence its labour laws will be founded. . . . Any house, unless it be a public monument, that does not come up to its rising standard of healthiness and convenience, the Utopian State will incontinently pull down, and pile the material and charge the owner for the labour; any house unduly crowded or dirty, it must in some effectual manner, directly or indirectly, confiscate and clear and clean. And any citizen indecently dressed, or ragged and dirty, or publicly unhealthy, or sleeping abroad homeless, or in any way

139 neglected or derelict, must/come under its care. It will find him work if he can and will work, it will take him to it, it will register him and lend him the money wherewith to lead a comely life until work can be found or made for him, and it will give him credit and shelter him and strengthen him if he is ill. In default of private enterprises it will provide inns for him and food, and it will — by itself acting as the reserve employer — maintain a minimum wage which will cover the cost of a decent life. The State will stand at the back of the economic struggle as the reserve employer of labour. . . .

140   The work publicly provided would have to be toilsome, but not cruel or incapacitating. A choice of occupations would need to be afforded. . . . Necessarily this employment by the State would be a relief of economic pressure, but it would not be considered a charity done to the individual, but a public service. . . .

There is a number of durable things bound finally to be useful that could be made and stored whenever the tide of more highly paid employment ebbed and labour sank to its minimum. . . . [N]ew roads could be made and public buildings reconstructed, inconveniences of all sorts removed, until under the stimulus of accumulating material, accumulating investments or other circumstances, the tide of private enterprise flowed again.

The State would provide these things for its citizen as though it was his right to require them. . . ./But 141 on the other hand it will require that the citizen who renders the minimum of service for these concessions shall not become a parent until he is established in work at a rate above the minimum, and free of any debt he may have incurred. The State will never press for its debt, nor put a limit to its accumulation so long as a man or woman remains childless; it will not even grudge them temporary spells of good fortune when they may lift their earnings above the minimum wage. It will pension the age of everyone who cares to take a pension, and it will maintain special guest homes for the very old to which they may come as paying guests, spending their pensions there. By such obvious devices it will achieve the maximum elimination of its feeble and spiritless folk in every generation with the minimum of suffering and public disorder.

But the mildly incompetent, the spiritless and dull, the poorer sort who are ill, do not exhaust our Utopian problem. There remain idiots and lunatics, there remain perverse and incompetent persons, there are people of weak character who become drunkards, drug/takers, and the like. Then there are persons 142 tainted with certain foul and transmissible diseases. . . . And there are violent people, and those who will not respect the property of others, thieves and cheats. . . . So soon as there can be no doubt of the disease or baseness of the individual, so soon as the insanity or other disease is assured, or the crime repeated a third time, or the drunkenness or misdemeanour past its seventh occasion (let us say), so soon must he or she pass out of the common ways of men. . . .

No doubt for first offenders, and for all offenders 143 under five-and-twenty, the Modern Utopia will attempt cautionary and remedial treatment. There will be disciplinary schools and colleges for the young. . . . But the others; what would a saner world do with them? . . . There would be no killing, no lethal chambers. No doubt Utopia will kill all deformed and monstrous and evilly diseased births, but for the rest, the State will hold itself accountable for their being. . . ./ Even for murder Utopia will not, I think, kill.   144

I doubt even if there will be jails. . . . Perhaps

islands will be chosen . . . and to these the State will send its exiles. . . . The State will, of course, secure itself against any children from these people, that is the primary object in their seclusion, and perhaps it may even be necessary to make these island prisons a system of island monasteries and island nunneries. . . .

About such islands patrol boats will go, there will be no freedoms of boat building, and it may be necessary to have armed guards at the creeks and quays. Be-
145 yond that the State will give these segregated/failures just as full a liberty as they can have. . . . The insane, of course, will demand care and control, but there is no reason why the islands of the hopeless drunkard, for example, should not each have a virtual autonomy. . . . I do not see why such an island should not build and order for itself and manufacture and trade. "Your ways are not our ways," the World State will say; "but here is freedom and a company of kindred souls. Elect your jolly rulers, brew if you will and distil; here are vine cuttings and barley fields; do as it pleases you to do." . . .

53-154   . . . [I]n a modern Utopia a man will/be free to be just as idle or uselessly busy as it pleases him, after he has earned the minimum wage. He must do that, of course, to pay for his keep, to pay his assurance tax against ill-health or old age, and any charge or debt paternity may have brought on him. The World State of the modern Utopist is no state of moral compulsions. If, for example, under the restricted Utopian scheme of inheritance, a man inherited sufficient money to release him from the need to toil, he would be free to go where he pleased and do what he liked.

. . . . .

180   . . . [I]t is time we faced the riddle of the problems of marriage and motherhood. . . .

The Modern Utopia is not only to be a sound and happy World State, but it is to be one progressing from good to better. . . . From the view of human comfort and happiness, the increase of population that occurs at each advance in human security is the great-
181 est evil of life. . . ./Progress depends essentially on competitive selection, and that we may not escape.

But it is a conceivable and possible thing that this margin of futile struggling, pain and discomfort and death might be reduced to nearly nothing . . . by preventing the birth of those who would in the unrestricted interplay of natural forces be born to suffer
182 and fail. . . ./The modern State . . . is taking over the responsibility of the general welfare of the children more and more, and as it does so, its right to decide which children it will shelter becomes more and more reasonable. . . .
183   . . . The State is justified in saying, before you

may add children to/the community for the commun- 184 ity to educate and in part to support, you must be above a certain minimum of personal efficiency, and this you must show by holding a position of solvency and independence in the world; you must be above a certain age, and a certain minimum of physical development, and free of any transmissible disease. You must not be a criminal unless you have expiated your offence. Failing these simple qualifications, if you and some person conspire and add to the population of the State, we will, for the sake of humanity, take over the innocent victim of your passions, but we shall insist that you are under a debt to the State of a peculiarly urgent sort, and one you will certainly pay, even if it is necessary to use restraint to get the payment out of you: it is a debt that has in the last resort your liberty as a security, and, moreover, if this thing happens a second time, or if it is disease or imbecility you have multiplied, we will take an absolutely effectual guarantee that neither you nor your partner offend again in this matter. . . .

But we may now come to the sexual aspects of 186 the modern ideal of a constitution of society in which, for all purposes of the individual, women are to be as free as men. . . ./[T]he Modern Utopia equalises 187 things between the sexes in the only possible way, by insisting that motherhood is a service to the State and/a legitimate claim to a living; and that, since the 188 State is to exercise the right of forbidding or sanctioning motherhood . . . the State secures to every woman who is, under legitimate sanctions, becoming or likely to become a mother, that is to say who is duly married, a certain wage from her husband to secure her against the need of toil and anxiety . . . it pays her a certain gratuity upon the birth of a child, and continues to pay at regular intervals sums sufficient to keep her and her child in independent freedom, so long as the child keeps up the minimum standard of health and physical and mental development. . . . [I]t pays more upon the child when it rises markedly above certain minimum qualifications, physical or mental, and, in fact, does its best to make thoroughly efficient motherhood a profession worth following. . . .

In Utopia a career of wholesome motherhood 189 would be, under such conditions as I have suggested, the normal and remunerative calling for a woman, and a capable woman who has borne, bred, and begun the education of eight or nine well-built, intelligent, and successful sons and daughters would be an extremely prosperous woman, quite irrespective of the economic fortunes of the man she has married. She would need to be an exceptional woman, and she would need to have chosen a man at least a little above the average as her partner in life. . . .

192   As a matter of justice, there must be no deception between the two people, and the State will ensure that in certain broad essentials this is so. . . . [E]ach would be supplied with a copy of the index card of the projected mate, on which would be recorded his or her age, previous marriages, legally important diseases, offspring, domiciles, public appointments, criminal convictions, registered assignments of property, and so

193 forth. . . ./In the event of the two people persisting in their resolution, they would . . . signify as much to the local official and the necessary entry would be made in the registers. These formalities would be quite independent of any religious ceremonial the contracting parties might choose, for with religious belief and procedure the modern State has no concern. . . . For those men and women who chose to ignore these conditions and to achieve any sort of union they liked the State would have no concern, unless offspring were born illegitimately. . . . [T]he further control of private morality, beyond the protection of the immature

194 from corruption and/evil example, will be no concern of the State's. . . .

198   The sound birth being assured, does there exist

199 any/valid reason for the persistence of the Utopian marriage union? . . . Children are the results of a choice between individuals; they grow well, as a rule, only in relation to sympathetic and kindred individualities, and no wholesale character-ignoring method of dealing with them has ever had a shadow of the suc-

200 cess of the individualised home. . . ./The balance of social advantage is certainly on the side of . . . permanent unions, on the side of an arrangement that, subject to ample provisions for a formal divorce without disgrace in cases of incompatibility, would bind, or at least enforce ideals that would tend to bind, a man and woman together for the whole term of her maternal activity, until, that is, the last born of her children was no longer in need of her help.

[In Wells' Utopia men are classified as Poietic, creative people who excel in imaginative activity; Kinetic, competent persons of less imagination who excel in administration; Dull, people of inadequate imagination, incompetent and imitative; and Base, egoists who do not contribute to and may even hinder the organization of the State. These types do not constitute social or hereditary classes; they are merely descriptive classifications.]

273   A modern Utopia differs from all the older Utopias in its recognition of the need of poietic activi-

274 ties. . . ./[T]he founders of this modern Utopia believed it possible to define conditions under which every individual born with poietic gifts should be enabled and encouraged to give them a full development,

in art, philosophy,/invention, or discovery. Certain 275 general conditions presented themselves as obviously reasonable: — to give every citizen as good an education as he or she could acquire, for example; to so frame it that the directed educational process would never at any period occupy the whole available time of the learner, but would provide throughout a marginal free leisure with opportunities for developing idiosyncracies, and to ensure by the expedient of a minimum wage for a specified amount of work, that leisure and opportunity did not cease throughout life.

But, in addition to thus making poietic activities universally possible, the founders of this modern Utopia sought to supply incentives . . . by which poietic men and women were given honour and enlarged freedoms, so soon as they produced an earnest of their quality. . . . There were great systems of laboratories attached to every municipal force station at which research could be conducted under the most favourable conditions, and every mine, and, indeed, almost every great industrial establishment, was saddled under its lease with similar obligations. . . . The World/State 276 tried the claims of every living contributor to any materially valuable invention, and paid or charged a royalty on its use that went partly to him personally, and partly to the research institution that had produced him. In the matter of literature and the philosophical and sociological sciences, every higher educational establishment carried its studentships, its fellowships, its occasional lectureships, and to produce a poem, a novel, a speculative work of force or merit, was to become the object of a generous competition between rival Universities. In Utopia, any author has the option either of publishing his works through the public bookseller as a private speculation, or, if he is of sufficient merit, of accepting a University endowment and conceding his copyright to the University press. All sorts of grants in the hands of committees of the most varied constitution, supplemented these academic resources, and ensured that no possible contributor to the wide flow of the Utopian mind slipped into neglect.

[The ruling class of the Modern Utopia, the Samurai, is described in a conversation between the author and one of its members.]

". . . Typically, the *samurai* are engaged in ad- 278 ministrative work. Practically the whole of the responsible rule of the world is in their hands; all our head teachers and disciplinary heads of colleges, our judges, barristers, employers of labour beyond a certain limit, practising medical men, legislators, must be *samurai*, and all the executive committees, and so forth, that play so large a part in our affairs are drawn by lot exclusively from them. The order is not hereditary. . . . The *samurai* are, in fact, volunteers. Any intelligent adult in a reasonably healthy and efficient state may, at any age after five-and-twenty, become one of the *samurai,* and take a hand in the universal control."

279   "Provided he follows the Rule."

    "Precisely — provided he follows the Rule. . . .

280 The Rule aims to exclude the dull and base/altogether, to discipline the impulses and emotions, to develop a moral habit and sustain a man in periods of stress, fatigue, and temptation, to produce the maximum co-operation of all men of good intent, and, in fact, to keep all the *samurai* in a state of moral and bodily health and efficiency. . . .

281   ". . . Our schooling period ends/now about four-teen, and a small number of boys and girls — about three per cent — are set aside then as unteachable, as, in fact, nearly idiotic; the rest go on to a college or upper school."

    "All your population?"

    "With that exception."

    "Free?"

    "Of course. And they pass out of college at eight-een. There are several different college courses, but one or other must be followed and a satisfactory ex-amination passed at the end — perhaps ten per cent fail — and the Rule requires that the candidate for the *samurai* must have passed."

    "But a very good man is sometimes an idle schoolboy."

    "We admit that. And so anyone who has failed to pass the college leaving examination may at any time in later life sit for it again — and again and again. . . .

284   ". . . Next to the intellectual qualification comes the
285 physical, the man must be in sound health,/free from certain foul, avoidable, and demoralising diseases, and in good training. We reject men who are fat, or thin and flabby, or whose nerves are shaky — we refer them back to training. And finally the man or woman must be fully adult . . . twenty-five for men and twenty-one for women. . . ."

    "And now, what is forbidden?"

286   "We forbid a good deal. . . . We prescribe a regimen of food, forbid tobacco, wine, or any alco-holic drink, all narcotic drugs — "

    "Meat?"

    "In all the round world of Utopia there is no meat. There used to be. But now we cannot stand the thought of slaughter-houses. . . .

287   "Originally the *samurai* were forbidden usury, that is to say the lending of money at fixed rates of interest. . . . The idea of a man growing richer by mere inaction and at the expense of an impoverishing debtor, is profoundly distasteful to Utopian ideas. . . . It is felt that to buy simply in order to sell again brings out many unsocial human qualities; it makes a man seek to enhance profits and falsify values, and so the *sam-urai* are forbidden to buy to sell on their own account or for any employer save the State, unless some pro-cess of manufacture changes the nature of the com-modity, . . . and they are forbidden salesmanship and all its arts. . . ."

    "But isn't there a vow of Chastity?" . . .   292

    "There is a Rule of Chastity here — but not of
Celibacy. . . ./A man under the Rule who loves a   294
woman who does not follow it, must either leave the *samurai* to marry her, or induce her to accept what is called the Woman's Rule, which, while it excepts her from the severer qualifications and disciplines, brings her regimen of life into a working harmony with his."

    "Suppose she breaks the Rule afterwards?"

    "He must leave either her or the order." . . .

Women *samurai* who are married . . . must bear   298
children — if they are to remain married as well as in the order — before the second period for terminating a childless marriage is exhausted. . . . There is one liberty accorded to women *samurai* which is refused to men, and that is to marry outside the Rule, and women married to men not under the Rule are also free to become *samurai.* . . ./Their children, as a rule,   299
become *samurai.* But it is not an exclusive caste . . . and so, unlike all other privileged castes the world has seen, it increases relatively to the total population, and may indeed at last assimilate almost the whole population of the earth. . . .

The leading principle of the Utopian religion is the repudiation of the doctrine of original sin; the/
Utopians hold that man, on the whole, is good. That   300
is their cardinal belief. . . .

Clearly the God of the *samurai* is a transcenden-   302
tal and mystical God. So far as the *samurai* have a purpose in common in maintaining the State, and the order and progress of the world, so far, by their discipline and denial, by their public work and effort, they worship God together. But the fount of motives lies in the individual life, it lies in silent and deliberate reflections, and at this, the most striking of all the rules of the *samurai* aims. For seven consecutive days in the year, at least, each man and woman under the/
Rule must go right out of all the life of man into some   303
wild and solitary place, must speak to no man or woman, and have no sort of intercourse with man-kind. . . . They must not go by beaten ways or wher-ever there are inhabited houses, but into the bare,

quiet places of the globe — the regions set apart for them. . . .

310 Practically all political power vests in the *sam-*
311 *urai.* Not only are they the only administrators,/law-yers, practising doctors, and public officials of almost all kinds, but they are the only voters. Yet, by a curious exception, the supreme legislative assembly must have one-tenth, and may have one-half of its members outside the order, because, it is alleged, there is a sort of wisdom that comes of sin and laxness, which is necessary to the perfect ruling of life. . . . The tendency is to give a practically permanent tenure to good men. Every ruler and official, it is true, is put on his trial every three years before a jury drawn by lot, according to the range of his activities, either from the *samurai* of his municipal area or from the general catalogue of the *samurai,* but the business of this jury is merely to decide whether to continue him in office or order a new election. In the majority of cases the verdict is continuation. Even if it is not so the official may still appear as a candidate before the second and separate jury which fills the vacant post.

. . . . .

TOPICS FOR SHORT PAPERS

The future of Wells' Utopia
Authority versus individual freedom in Wells' Utopia
The selection and duties of the *Samurai*
The elimination of the inferior in Wells' Utopia
Some aspects of Wells' Utopia which are in force in twentieth-century America

EXERCISE

A. A proper topic outline begins with a thesis sentence. The first paragraph of the selection from *A Modern Utopia* contains an idea central to Wells' conception of the ideal state. Formulate this idea as a thesis sentence and construct a topic outline of these excerpts which will show how Wells develops and demonstrates this central idea as he discusses various aspects of his Utopia.

B. "The Utopia of a modern dreamer must needs differ in one fundamental aspect from the Nowheres and Utopias men planned before Darwin quickened the thought of the world. Those were all perfect and static states, a balance of happiness won for ever against the forces of unrest and disorder that inhere in things. . . . Change

and development were dammed back by invincible dams for ever. But the Modern Utopia must not be static but kinetic, must shape not as a permanent state but as a hopeful stage, leading to a long ascent of stages. Nowadays we do not resist and overcome the great stream of things, but rather float upon it." — H. G. Wells, *A Modern Utopia,* p. 5.

Construct an outline for a paper which will investigate the validity of this statement by comparing Wells' Utopia with one other ideal state. Remember that a proper topic outline begins with a thesis sentence. Then, following your outline, develop your thesis sentence in a 400-word paper.

A SELECTED BIBLIOGRAPHY

Beach, Joseph Warren. *The Twentieth Century Novel.* New York and London, 1932, pp. 65-74.

Hyde, W. J. "The Socialism of H. G. Wells in the Early Twentieth Century," *Journal of the History of Ideas,* XVII (1956), 217-234.

Joad, C. E. M. "An Open Letter to H. G. Wells," *New Statesman and Nation,* Aug. 17, 1940, pp. 154-155; reply by H. G. Wells, Aug. 24, 1940, p. 180; reply by C. E. M. Joad, Aug. 31, 1940, p. 208.

Lee, Vernon. "On Modern Utopias. An Open Letter to H. G. Wells," *Fortnightly Review,* n.s. LXXX (1906), 1123-1137.

Macy, John. "H. G. Wells and Utopia," in *The Critical Game.* New York, 1922, pp. 269-276.

Murry, John Middleton. "Art and Society: H. G. Wells and the Collective Ideal," *Arts,* XIV (1928), 101-125.

Nicholson, Norman. *H. G. Wells.* London, 1950.

Pease, Edward R. "The Episode of Mr. Wells," in *The History of the Fabian Society.* Rev. ed. New York, 1926, pp. 163-184.

Stewart, Herbert L. "The Prophetic Office of Mr. H. G. Wells," *International Journal of Ethics,* XXX (1920), 172-189.

Wells, H. G. "Project of a World Society," *New Statesman and Nation,* Aug. 20, 1932, pp. 197-198.

West, Geoffrey [pseud. Geoffrey Harry Wells]. *H. G. Wells.* New York, 1930.

SUBJECTS FOR LIBRARY PAPERS

The socialism of H. G. Wells
The prophetic romances of H. G. Wells

SKINNER: Walden Two

B. F. Skinner. WALDEN TWO. New York: The Macmillan Company, 1948.

B. F. Skinner (1904 —), psychologist and teacher, wrote Walden Two *in 1948. Although it is too early to assess its place in the development of Utopian literature, it is notable for the belief that in the recently formulated behavioristic psychology man has a means of conditioning himself to accept the good life which is available to him.*

Walden Two is an experimental community of about one thousand people, located on farmland somewhere in the contemporary United States and conceived and put into operation by T. E. Frazier, a psychologist. To this community come six visitors: Professor Burris, another psychologist and the "I" of the novel; Professor Castle, a teacher of philosophy; and four young people, Rodge Rogers, Steve Jamnik, Barbara Macklin, and Mary Grove. This selection begins after Frazier has conducted the group on a tour of the buildings and lands of Walden Two.

40   "We are grateful for your kindness," I said to Frazier, "not only in asking us to visit Walden Two but in giving us so much of your time. I'm afraid it's something of an imposition."

"On the contrary," said Frazier. "I'm fully paid for talking with you. Two labor-credits are allowed each day for taking charge of guests of Walden Two. . . ."

"Labor-credits?" I said.

"I'm sorry. I had forgotten. Labor-credits are a sort of money. But they're not coins or bills — just entries in a ledger. All goods and services are free. . . . Each of us pays for what he uses with twelve hundred labor-credits each year — say, four credits for each workday. We change the value according to the needs of the community. . . . All we ask is to make expenses, with a slight margin of safety; we adjust the value of the labor-credit accordingly. At present it's about one hour of work per credit."

"Your members work only four hours a day?" I said. . . .

41   "On the average," Frazier replied casually. . . . "A credit system also makes it possible to evaluate a job in terms of the willingness of the members to undertake it. After all, a man isn't doing more or less than his share because of the time he puts in; it's what he's doing that counts. So we simply assign different credit values to different kinds of work, and adjust them from time to time on the basis of demand. . . ."

"An unpleasant job like cleaning sewers has a high value, I suppose," I said.

"Exactly. Somewhere around one and a half credits per hour. . . . Pleasanter jobs have lower values — say point seven or point eight. . . . In the long run, when the values have been adjusted, all kinds of work are equally desirable. If they weren't, there would be a demand for the more desirable, and the credit value would be changed. . . ."

"What about the knowledge and skill required in many jobs?" said Castle. "Doesn't that interfere with free bidding? Certainly you can't allow just anyone to work as a doctor."

"No, of course not. The principle has to be modi- 42 fied where long training is needed. Still, the preferences of the community as a whole determine the final value. If our doctors were conspicuously overworked *according to our standards,* it would be hard to get young people to choose that profession. We must see to it that there are enough doctors to bring the average schedule within range of the Walden Two standard."

"What if nobody wanted to be a doctor?" I said.

"Our trouble is the other way round."

"I thought as much," said Castle. "Too many of your young members will want to go into interesting lines in spite of the work load. What do you do, then?"

"Let them know how many places will be available, and let them decide. . . . The fact is, it's very unlikely that anyone at Walden Two will set his heart on a course of action so firmly that he'll be unhappy if it isn't open to him. . . . The chances are that our superfluous young premedic will find other courses open to him which will very soon prove equally attractive."

"There's another case, too," I said. "You must have some sort of government. I don't see how you can permit a free choice of jobs there."

"Our only government is a Board of Planners," said Frazier. . . . "There are six Planners, usually three men and three women. The sexes are on such equal terms here/that no one guards equality very jealously. They may serve for ten years, but no longer. . . .

43 "The Planners are charged with the success of the community. They make policies, review the work of the Managers, keep an eye on the state of the nation in general. They also have certain judicial functions. They're allowed six hundred credits a year for their services, which leaves two credits still due each day. At least one must be worked out in straight physical labor. . . ."

"How do you choose your Planners?" said Rodge.

"The Board selects a replacement from a pair of names supplied by the Managers."

"The members don't vote for them?" said Castle.

"*No,*" said Frazier emphatically.

"What are Managers?" I said hastily.

"What the name implies: specialists in charge of the divisions and services of Walden Two. . . . They requisition labor according to their needs, and their job is the managerial function which survives after they've assigned as much as possible to others. . . . It's an exceptional person who seeks and finds a place as Manager. . . ."

"*They* are elected by the members, I suppose?" said Castle. . . .

"The Managers aren't honorific personages, but carefully trained and tested specialists. How could the members gauge their ability? No, these are very much like Civil Service jobs. You work up to be a Manager — through intermediate positions which carry a good deal of responsibility and provide the necessary apprenticeship."

"Then the members have no voice whatsoever," said Castle. . . .

"Nor do they wish to have," said Frazier flatly. . . . 44

"Then you distinguish only Planners, Managers, and Workers," I said. . . .

"And Scientists. The community supports a certain amount of research. Experiments are in progress in plant and animal breeding, the control of infant behavior, educational processes of several sorts, and the use of some of our raw materials. Scientists receive the same labor-credits as Managers — two or three per day depending upon the work."

"No pure science?" exclaimed Castle with mock surprise.

"Only in our spare time," said Frazier. . . .

"Why should everyone engage in menial work?" 45 I asked. "Isn't that really a misuse of manpower if a man has special talents or abilities?"

"There's no misuse. Some of us would be smart enough to get along without doing physical work, but we're also smart enough to know that in the long run it would mean trouble. A leisure class would grow like a cancer until the strain on the rest of the community became intolerable. We might escape the consequences in our own lifetime, but we couldn't visualize a permanent society on such a plan. . . .

"But there's a better reason why brains must not 46 neglect brawn," Frazier continued. "Nowadays it's the smart fellow, the small-muscle user, who finds himself in the position of governor. . . . In work of this sort the manager must keep an eye on the managed, must understand his needs, must experience his lot. That's why our Planners, Managers, and Scientists are required to work out some of their labor-credits in menial tasks."

. . . . .

Frazier entered upon a discussion of economics. 64 The community was not, of course, completely self-sufficient. It needed certain materials and equipment and had to buy power and pay taxes. Hence it/had to 65 create "foreign exchange." At the moment this was apparently not satisfactory. The community had not yet made the best use of its supply of skilled labor. But several small industries were already well-established and others were being worked out. The community was paying its way, but Frazier felt that it could be done more efficiently.

. . . . .

"Somehow or other," said Frazier . . . "you have 71 avoided the most fatuous of all our visitors' questions. 'If you don't work, then whatever do you do with all your time?' . . ."

". . . Pardon me for being fatuous [said Castle], but what *do* you do with all your time?" . . .

"Take music, for example. . . . If you live in 73

Walden Two and like music, you may go as far as you like. I don't mean a few minutes a day — I mean all the time and energy you can give to music and remain healthy. If you want to listen, there's an extensive library of records and, of course, many concerts, some of them quite professional. All the good radio programs are broadcast over the system of loudspeakers that we call the Walden Network, and they are monitored to remove the advertising.

"If you want to perform, you can get instruction on almost any instrument from other members — who 75 get credits for it. . . ./And remember, we aren't specializing in music, either. . . . We don't specialize in anything. We have time for everything. I could tell you a similar story for painting and sculpture and half a dozen applied arts."

[Frazier next conducts his visitors on a tour of the schools of Walden Two, beginning with the nursery.]

77 A young woman in a white uniform met us in a small waiting room near the entrance. . . .

"I hope Mr. Frazier has warned you," she said with a smile, "that we're going to be rather impolite and give you only a glimpse of our babies. We try to protect them from infection during the first year. It's especially important when they're cared for as a group."

78 "What about the parents?" said Castle at once. "Don't parents see their babies?"

"Oh, yes, so long as they are in good health. Some parents work in the nursery. Others come around every day or so, for at least a few minutes. They take the baby out for some sunshine, or play with it in a play room." Mrs. Nash smiled at Frazier. "That's the way we build up the baby's resistance," she added.

She opened a door and allowed us to look into a small room, three walls of which were lined with cubicles, each with a large glass window. Behind the windows we could see babies of various ages. None of them wore more than a diaper, and there were no bedclothes. In one cubicle a small red newborn was asleep on its stomach. Some of the older babies were awake and playing with toys. . . .

79 "But why don't you put clothes on them?" said Barbara.

"What for? It would mean laundry for us and discomfort for the child. It's the same with sheets and blankets. Our babies lie on a stretched plastic cloth which doesn't soak up moisture and can be wiped clean in a moment." . . .

"When a baby graduates from our Lower Nursery," Frazier broke in, "it knows nothing of frustration, anxiety, or fear. It never cries except when sick,

which is very seldom, and it has a lively interest in everything."

"But is it prepared for life?" said Castle. "Surely you can't continue to protect it from frustration or frightening situations forever."

"Of course not. But it can be prepared for them. We can build a tolerance for frustration by introducing obstacles gradually as the baby grows strong enough to handle them. . . ./We introduce annoyances 80 slowly, according to the ability of the baby to take them. It's very much like innoculation. . . .

"As to emotions [Frazier continued] — we aren't 83 free of them all, nor should we like to be. But the meaner and more annoying — the emotions which breed unhappiness — are almost unknown here, like unhappiness itself. . . ./[W]hen a particular emotion is 84 no longer a useful part of a behavioral repertoire, we proceed to eliminate it."

"Yes, but how?"

"It's simply a matter of behavioral engineering," said Frazier.

[Frazier then explains the methods of behavioral engineering.]

"Take the principle of 'Get thee behind me, Sa- 87 tan,' for example. . . . It's a special case of self-control by altering the environment. Subclass A3, I believe. We give each child a lollipop which has been dipped in powdered sugar so that a single touch of the tongue can be detected. We tell him he may eat the lollipop later in the day, provided it hasn't already been licked. Since the child is only three or four, it is a fairly diff — "

"Three or four!" Castle exclaimed.

"All our ethical training is completed by the age of six," said Frazier quietly. "A simple principle like putting temptation out of sight would be acquired before four. But at such an early age the problem of not licking the lollipop isn't easy. Now, what would you do, Mr. Castle, in a similar situation?"

"Put the lollipop out of sight as quickly as pos- 88 sible."

"Exactly. I can see you've been well trained. . . . First of all, the children are urged to examine their own behavior while looking at the lollipops. This helps them to recognize the need for self-control. Then the lollipops are concealed, and the children are asked to notice any gain in happiness or any reduction in tension. Then a strong distraction is arranged — say, an interesting game. Later the children are reminded of the candy and encouraged to examine their reaction. The value of the distraction is generally obvious. . . . When the experiment is repeated a day or so later, the children all run with the lollipops to their lockers and do exactly what Mr. Castle would do — a sufficient indication of the success of our training. . . . In a later experiment the children wear their lollipops like crucifixes for a few hours." . . .

"How do you build up a tolerance to an annoying situation?" I said.

"Oh, for example, by having the children 'take' a more and more painful shock, or drink cocoa with 89 less and less sugar in it/until a bitter concoction can be savored without a bitter face."

"But jealousy or envy — you can't administer them in graded doses," I said.

"And why not? Remember, we control the social environment, too, at this age. . . . Take this case. A group of children arrive home after a long walk tired and hungry. They're expecting supper; they find, instead, that it's time for a lesson in self-control: they must stand for five minutes in front of steaming bowls of soup. . . . One of them may make a joke of it. . . . Another may start a song with many verses. . . . It's a rather severe biological frustration, for the children are tired and hungry and they must stand and look at food; but it's passed off as lightly as a five-minute delay at curtain time. . . . In a later stage we forbid all social devices. No songs, no jokes — merely silence. Each child is forced back upon his own resources — a very important step.

90 ". . . A still more/advanced stage . . . brings me to my point. When it's time to sit down to the soup, the children count off — heads and tails. Then a coin is tossed and if it comes up heads, the 'heads' sit down and eat. The 'tails' remain standing for another five minutes." . . .

"And you call that envy?" I said.

"Perhaps not exactly," said Frazier. "At least there's seldom any aggression against the lucky ones. The emotion, if any, is directed against Lady Luck herself, against the toss of the coin. That, in itself, is a lesson worth learning, for it's the only direction in which emotion has a surviving chance to be useful. . . . Its expression is not socially objectionable. . . .

"After all, it's a simple and sensible program," he went on. . . . "We set up a system of gradually increasing annoyances and frustrations against a background of complete serenity. An easy environment is made more and more difficult as the children acquire 93 the capacity to adjust. . . ./We make every man a brave man. They all come over the barriers. Some require more preparation than others, but they all come over. The traditional use of adversity is to select the strong. We control adversity to build strength. And we do it deliberately . . . in order to prepare for adversities which are beyond control. Our children eventually experience the 'heartache and the thousand natural shocks that flesh is heir to.' It would be the cruelest possible practice to protect them as long as possible, especially when we *could* protect them so well." . . .

The living quarters and daily schedules of the 95 older children furnished a particularly good example of behavioral engineering. . . . The children passed smoothly from one age group to another, following a natural process of growth and avoiding the abrupt changes of the home-and-school system. The arrangements were such that each child emulated children slightly older than himself and hence derived motives and patterns for much of his early education without adult aid.

The control of the physical and social environment . . . was progressively relaxed. . . . After spending most of the first year in an air-conditioned cubicle, and the second and third mainly in an air-conditioned room with a minimum of clothing and bedding, the three- or four-year-old was introduced to regular clothes and given the care of a small standard cot in a dormitory. The beds of the five- and six-year-olds were grouped by threes and fours in a series of alcoves furnished like rooms and treated as such by the children. Groups of three or four seven-year-olds occupied small rooms together, and this practice was continued, with frequent changes of roommates, until the children were about thirteen, at which time they took temporary rooms in the adult building, usually in pairs. At marriage, or whenever the individual chose, he could participate in building a larger room for himself or refurnishing an old room which might be available. . . .

We visited some of the workshops, laboratories, 96 studies, and reading rooms used in lieu of classrooms. They were occupied, but it was not entirely clear that the children were actually in school. I supposed that the few adults to be seen about the building were teachers, but . . . more often than not they were busy with some private business. . . . I had to admit that an enormous amount of learning was probably going on, but I had never seen a school like it before. . . . The doors and many of the windows stood open, and a fair share of the schoolwork, or whatever it was, took place outside. Children were constantly passing in and out. . . . Everyone seemed to be enjoying extraordinary freedom, but the efficiency and comfort of the whole group were preserved. . . .

"We can arrange things more expeditiously here 97 because we don't need to be constantly re-educating [Frazier said]. . . . We don't need 'grades.' Everyone knows that talents and abilities don't develop at the same rate in different children. . . . Here the child advances as rapidly as he likes in any field. No time is wasted in forcing him to participate in, or be bored by, activities he has outgrown. And the backward child can be handled more efficiently too.

"We also don't require all our children to develop the same abilities or skills. We don't insist upon a certain set of courses. I don't suppose we have a single child who has had a 'secondary school education,' whatever that means. But they've all developed as rapidly as advisable, and they're well-educated in many useful respects. By the same token we don't waste time in teaching the/unteachable. . . . 98

"Since our children remain happy, energetic, and curious, we don't need to teach 'subjects' at all. We teach only the techniques of learning and thinking. As for geography, literature, the sciences — we give our children opportunity and guidance, and they learn them for themselves. . . . Our children aren't neglected, but they're seldom, if ever, *taught* anything.

". . . Our children begin to work at a very early age. It's no hardship; it's accepted as readily as sport or play. And a good share of our education goes on in workshops, laboratories, and fields. It's part of the Walden Two Code to encourage children in all the arts and crafts. . . ."

"What about higher education?" I said.

"We aren't equipped for professional training, of course," said Frazier. "Those who want to go on to graduate study in a university are given special preparation. . . ./We give them an excellent survey of the methods and techniques of thinking, taken from logic, statistics, scientific method, psychology, and mathematics. That's all the 'college education' they need. . . ." 99

"But what about libraries and laboratories, though?" I said. . . .

"As to a library, we pride ourselves on having the best books, if not the most. . . . Our laboratories are good because they are real. Our workshops are really small engineering laboratories. . . . We teach anatomy in the slaughterhouse, botany in the field, genetics in the dairy and poultry house, chemistry in the medical building and in the kitchen and dairy laboratory. What more can you ask?"

. . . . .

106   Just south of the flower gardens, on a blanket spread out upon the warm grass, lay a naked baby nine or ten months old. A boy and girl were trying to make her crawl toward a rubber doll. . . . Frazier said casually, "Their first child."

"Good heavens!" I cried. "Do you mean to say those children are the parents of that baby? . . . But they can't be more than sixteen or seventeen years old!"

"Probably not."

"But isn't that rather remarkable? It's not the usual thing, I hope." . . .

"It's not at all unusual with us," Frazier said. . . .

"Do girls have babies as easily when they are so young, though?" said Barbara. 109

"Easier," said Frazier flatly. . . . "We make sure, of course, that the girl is capable of normal childbearing, but we should do that at any age."

"How long does she go on having babies?"

"As long as she likes, but generally no longer than usual. If she wants four children, say, she will be finished with childbearing by the time she's twenty-two or -three. . . . At twenty-three she will find herself as young in body and spirit as if she had spent the same years unmarried. Her adult life opens up to her with many interesting prospects. For one thing, she is then quite on a par with men. She has made the special contribution which is either the duty or the privilege of woman, and can take her place without distinction of sex. . . . There are scarcely any types of work which are not shared equally." . . .

"But isn't there one trouble?" said Barbara. "Do 110 young people really know what kind of person they want to live with for the rest of their lives?" . . .

". . . [L]et me add a scientific touch. When a 111 young couple become engaged, they go to our Manager of Marriages. Their interests, school records, and health are examined. If there's any great discrepancy in intellectual ability or temperament they are advised against marrying. The marriage is at least postponed, and that usually means it's abandoned." . . .

"Are you conducting any genetic experiments?" 112 I said.

"No," said Frazier, but he sat up straight as if the subject were especially interesting. "We discourage childbearing by the unfit,/of course, but that's all. You 113 must remember that we've only recently reached our present size, and even so, we aren't large enough for serious experimentation. Later, perhaps, something can be done. The weakening of the family structure will make experimental breeding possible. . . .

"Walden Two replaces the family, not only as 114 an economic unit, but to some extent as a social and psychological unit as well [Frazier continued]. . . ./ We make a great deal of the 'engagement.' In the 116 world at large this is a statement of intention and a period of trial. It's that with us. The young couple receive medical and psychological counsel during this period. . . . Our marriage ceremony is unambiguous, and I'm sure it's entered into in good faith. If in the course of time extramarital friendships weaken the original tie, we try to avoid an open break. A disinterested person, usually one of our psychologists, gives immediate counsel and guidance. Frequently the matter straightens itself out, and the original tie is preserved. But if the old affection is quite dead and the new one genuine, a divorce is carried through. . . ."

117   "What about the children?" I said. "The group care we saw this morning must also weaken the relation between parent and child."

"It does. By design. We have to attenuate the child-parent relation. . . . Home is not the place to raise children. Even when our young mothers and fathers become skilled nursery-school workers, we avoid a strong personal dependency. Our goal is to have every adult member of Walden Two regard all our children as his own, and to have every child think of every adult as his parent. . . .

118   "The weakening of the relation between parent and child is valuable in other ways," Frazier con-
119 tinued. . . ./"When divorce cannot be avoided, the children are not embarrassed by severe changes in their way of life or their behavior toward their parents. It's also easy to induce the unfit or unwell to forego parenthood. No stigma attaches to being childless, and no lack of affection. That's what I meant when I said that experiments in selective breeding would eventually be possible in Walden Two. The hereditary connection will be minimized to the point of being forgotten. Long before that, it will be possible to breed through artificial insemination without altering the personal relation of husband and wife. Our people will marry as they wish, but have children according to a genetic plan."

. . . . .

135   ". . . [H]ere's the crux of the whole question of community life: how can you put such a program into effect?"

"It's really not so hard as the Philistines have supposed," said Frazier. "We have certain rules of conduct, the Walden Code, which are changed from time to time as experience suggests. . . . Each member agrees to abide by the Code when he accepts membership. That's what he gives in return for his constitutional guarantee of a share in the wealth and life of the community. The Code acts as a memory aid until good behavior becomes habitual." . . .

136   "But why do you all continue to observe the Code?" I said. "Isn't there a natural drift away from it? Or simple disagreement?"

"As to disagreement, anyone may examine the evidence upon which a rule was introduced into the Code. He may argue against its inclusion and may present his own evidence. If the Managers refuse to change the rule, he may appeal to the Planners. But in no case must he argue about the Code with the members at large. There's a rule against that."

"I would certainly argue against the inclusion of *that* rule," said Castle. "Simple democracy requires public discussion of so fundamental a matter as a code."

"You won't find very much 'simple democracy' here," said Frazier casually. . . . "As to any drifting away from the Code, that's prevented by the very techniques which the Managers use to gain observance in the first place. The rules are frequently brought to the attention of the members. Groups of rules are discussed from time to time in our weekly meetings. The advantages for the community are pointed out and specific applications are described. In some cases simple rules are appropriately posted."

. . . . .

"We are opposed to personal competition [Fra-140 zier said]. . . . We never mark any member for special approbation. There must be some other source of satisfaction in one's work or play, or we regard an achievement as quite trivial. . . . Our decision to eliminate personal aggrandizement arose quite naturally from the fact that we were thinking about the whole group. We could not see how the group could gain from individual glory." . . .

"What's left to motivate your workers?" I said. 142 "Take a Manager, for example. He doesn't work for money — that's out. He doesn't work for personal acclaim — that's forbidden. What's left? I suppose you'd say he works to avoid the consequences of failure. . . ."

"I wouldn't say that. We don't condemn a man for poor work. After all, if we don't praise him, it would be unfair to blame him."

"You mean you would let an incompetent man continue to do a poor job?" said Castle.

"By no means. He would be given other work, 143 and a competent man brought in. But he wouldn't be blamed."

"For heaven's sake, why not?" said Castle.

"Do you blame a man for getting sick?"

"Of course not."

"But poor work by a capable man is a form of illness. . . . A moral or ethical lapse, whether in explicit violation of the Code or not, needs treatment, not punishment."

"You merely offer your condolences for a mild case of larceny?" said Castle.

"No, condolences are out too. The doctor seldom expresses sympathy for his patient — and wisely, I think. We simply treat the illness as an objective fact." . . .

"But what if a man did poor work, or none at all, in every job you put him on?" said Castle.

"The disease would be judged quite serious, and the man would be sent to one of our psychologists."

. . . . .

161 "The one fact that I would cry from every housetop is this: the Good Life is waiting for us — here and now! [Frazier said] . . . It doesn't depend upon a change in government or on the machinations of world politics. It doesn't wait upon an improvement in human nature. At this very moment we have the necessary techniques, both material and psychological, to create a full and satisfying life for everyone."

"The trick is to put those techniques into effect," said Castle. "You still have to solve the practical problems of government and politics."

"Government and politics! It's not a problem of government and politics at all. That's the first plank in the Walden Two platform. You can't make progress toward the Good Life by political action! . . . You must operate on another level entirely. What you need is a sort of Nonpolitical Action Committee: keep out of politics and away from government except for practical and temporary purposes. . . ."

163 "It sounds a little like the old program of anarchy," said Castle.

"By no means. I'm not arguing for no government at all, but only for none of the existing forms. We want a government based upon a science of human behavior. Nothing short of that will produce a permanent social structure. For the first time in history we're ready for it, because we can now deal with human behavior in accordance with simple scientific principles. . . . We can *make* men adequate for group living — to the satisfaction of everybody. That was our faith, but now it's a fact." . . .

165 "I have been meaning to ask about religious practices," I said. . . .

"Walden Two isn't a religious community. . . . We don't give our children any religious training, though parents are free to do so if they wish. Our conception of man is not taken from theology but from a scientific examination of man himself. And we recognize no revealed truths about good or evil or the laws or codes of a successful society.

"The simple fact is, the religious practices which our members brought to Walden Two have fallen away

166 little by little. . . ./We have no need for formal religion, either as ritual or philosophy. But I think we're a devout people in the best sense of that word, and we're far better behaved than any thousand church members taken at random.

"We've borrowed some of the practices of organized religion — to inspire group loyalty and strengthen the observance of the Code. I believe I've mentioned our Sunday meetings. There's usually some sort of music, sometimes religious. And a philosophical, poetic, or religious work is read or acted out. . . . Then there's a brief 'lesson' — of the utmost importance in maintaining an observance of the Code. Usually items are chosen for discussion which deal with self-control and certain kinds of social articulation.

"There's nothing spurious about this — it's not an imitation church service, and our members aren't fooled. The music serves the same purpose as in a church — it makes the service enjoyable and establishes a mood. The weekly lesson is a sort of group therapy. And it seems to be all we need. If the Code is too difficult for anyone or doesn't seem to be working to his advantage, he seeks the help of our psychologists. They're our 'priests,' if you like. The treatments prescribed are very much like those of the psychological clinic except that the disorders are almost always comparatively minor and the therapy therefore usually successful."

. . . . .

"What about your elite? Isn't that a Fascist de- 194 vice?" said Castle. "Isn't it true that your Planners and Managers exercise a sort of control which is denied to the common member?"

"But only because that control is necessary for the proper functioning of the community. Certainly our elite do not command a disproportionate share of the wealth of the community; on the contrary, they work rather harder, I should say, for what they get. . . .

"A dominant figure in Walden Two is quite un- 195 thinkable," said Frazier. "The culture which has emerged from our experiments doesn't require strong personal leadership. On the contrary, it contains several checks and guarantees against it. As I explained before, no one in Walden Two ever acts for the benefit of anyone else except as the agent of the community. Personal favoritism . . . has been destroyed by our cultural engineers. No one is ever in debt to any figure, or any group short of the/whole community." 196

TOPICS FOR SHORT PAPERS

The principles and practice of behavioral engineering in Walden Two

Leadership in Walden Two

The relative emphasis on science and art in Skinner's educational scheme

The significance of Walden Two's difference in place and time from other theoretical Utopias

Duties of the members of Walden Two

EXERCISE

A. In one of the above excerpts Burris asks Frazier how workers are motivated to serve Walden Two. Frazier does not specifically answer this question in the discussion in which it is asked, nor does he specifically answer it anywhere in the novel.

Take précis notes on the passages in *Walden Two* which concern the duties of the members. Use these précis notes to construct an outline of a paper which will answer Burris's question.

B. Use your précis notes on *Walden Two* along with the notes you have taken on the same subject from Bellamy's *Looking Backward* to construct an outline for a paper on this topic: Duties of citizens in Bellamy's society and in Skinner's Walden Two. Be sure to begin by formulating a thesis sentence. Then, drawing on your notes alone and following your outline, develop your thesis sentence in a 500-word paper.

A SELECTED BIBLIOGRAPHY

Bernard, L. L. "The Psychological Foundations of Society," in *Introduction to Sociology*, ed. Jerome Davis and Harry Elmer Barnes. New York, 1927, pp. 397-491.

Hacker, Andrew. "Dostoevsky's Disciples: Men and Sheep in Political Theory," *Journal of Politics*, XVII (1955), 590-613.

Krutch, Joseph Wood. "Ignoble Utopias," in *The Measure of Man*. Indianapolis, 1954, pp. 55-76.

"Skinner, Prof. B[urrhus] F[rederic]." *American Men of Science*, ed. Jaques Cattell. 9th ed. 3 vols. New York, 1956, III, 626.

Skinner, B. F. "Freedom and the Control of Men," *American Scholar*, XXV (1955), 47-65. Reprinted in *Perspectives USA*, XV (1956), 104-121.

Watson, John B. *Behaviorism*. New York, 1925.

Williams, Donald C. "The Social Scientist as Philosopher and King," *Philosophical Review*, LVIII (1949), 345-359.

SUBJECTS FOR LIBRARY PAPERS

Walden Two and Behaviorism

Critics and Defenders of the Social Order of *Walden Two* (Begin by reading reviews of the book and Krutch's essay in *The Measure of Man*.)

Appendix

TOPICS FOR CONTROLLED RESEARCH PAPERS

1. Types of government
2. The authority of the state
3. The status of the individual
4. The creation of a ruling class
5. The duties of a ruling class
6. The duties of ordinary citizens
7. The care of the incapable
8. The treatment of the criminal and the lazy
9. Communal ownership and private property
10. Distribution of goods and services
11. Wages
12. Opportunities for advancement
13. The conditions of labor
14. The use of leisure time
15. The place and purpose of art, music, and literature
16. Science and technology
17. Religion
18. Eugenics
19. Legislature and courts
20. War: waging and preventing
21. Political and economic relations with other nations
22. The status of women
23. Courtship, marriage, and the family
24. Rearing children
25. The methods of education
26. The purposes of education
27. The character of Utopian man
28. An underlying basis of several Utopian schemes